A STEP-BY-STEP GUIDE TO GIVING YOUR CHILD
A PROFESSIONAL LOOKING HAIRCUT AT HOME

HOW TO CUT YOUR CHILD'S HAIR AT HOME

W9-CBG-575

HOW TO CUT YOUR CHILD'S HAIR AT HOME

A STEP-BY-STEP GUIDE TO GIVING YOUR CHILD
A PROFESSIONAL LOOKING HAIRCUT AT HOME

Laura DeRosa

Illustrations by
Judy Love

Avery Publishing Group
Garden City Park, New York

Cover Design: William Gonzalez and Rudy Shur
Cover Art: Jürek, Provincetown, Massachusetts
Text Illustrations: Judy Love
In-House Editor: Marie Caratozzolo
Typesetter: Bonnie Freid
Printer: Paragon Press, Honesdale, Pennsylvania

Library of Congress Cataloging-in-Publication Data

DeRosa, Laura Hinckley.
    How to cut your child's hair at home : a simple guide to giving
your child a professional-looking haircut at home / by Laura
Hinckley DeRosa.
        p. cm.
    Includes index.
    ISBN 0-89529-612-8
    1. Haircutting.   I. Title.
TT970.D464   1994
646.7'242—dc20   94-10817
                                                        CIP

Copyright © 1994 by Laura Hinckley DeRosa

Printed in the United States of America

10 9 8 7 6 5 4 3 2 1

Contents

To my children—
Joseph, Brian, and Jacqueline

Acknowledgments

For all of their help and encouragement, I would like to extend my thanks to the following family and friends:

My mother, Pat Hinckley
My sisters, Kelly Sampson and Michelle Vella
My sister-in-law, Jean Hinckley
My friends Kym Caslin and Dawn Maly

For their input, I would like to acknowledge my co-workers—Ginny, Robert, Jen, Donna, and Mark.

Thank you to my illustrator, Judy Love, and to all of the children who modeled for the pictures—Jaci, Joey, Brian, Tom, and Andrea.

I am grateful to my publisher, Rudy Shur, for having faith in this project, and to my editor, Marie Caratozzolo, for her editorial guidance.

Thanks also goes to Shirley Moscow, who guided me through the publishing process.

Finally, a special thanks to my husband, Rob DeRosa, for his tolerance and for giving up so much of our time together so that I could write this book.

Introduction

Have you ever tried to cut your child's hair but ended up with "less than perfect" results? Maybe you have taken your child to a salon only to be told, "I'm sorry, I can't cut his hair if he won't sit still." As I am both a parent and a professional hairstylist, I know this happens quite often, especially with children under three years old. To expect a young child to sit for twenty minutes or so while a stranger cuts his or her hair is asking a lot. And even if your child sits still during a haircut, you may not like the style of the cut he or she receives.

There is probably no one who is better suited to cut your child's hair than you are. As a parent, you know the look you want your child to have, and you know best how to deal with his or her behavior. With a little guidance, you can learn how to cut your child's hair correctly.

There will always be those people who attempt to cut their children's hair at home. If you are one of these people, this book is for you. A simple, logical method for cutting hair is presented for a variety of basic styles. Once you become familiar with the method, you should have no problem giving your child a good haircut in a half hour or so.

You have the option of choosing a good time to give the

haircut—morning, noon, or night. The best time, of course, is when you are relaxed and can take your time. Rushing causes stress, which, in turn, can make your child anxious and less cooperative.

Your friends will marvel at your ability to keep your child's hair looking its best at all times. You can be in complete control of the way your child's hair looks—not at the mercy of stylists who may do what they want, rather than what you want.

Your child is never too young to have his or her hair styled. A spray of water and a comb can do wonders for baby's flyaway hair. A little "trim around the edges" can make a one-year-old look put together. Furthermore, if you start fixing children's hair at an early age, they will be used to it. Hair care, like brushing teeth, will become a natural part of their routine.

When you give your child that first haircut yourself, don't be discouraged if the results are not perfect. Giving good haircuts comes with experience. Until you feel confident in your ability, pick a time to cut your child's hair when it won't interfere with things like holidays or school pictures. You don't want to put any unnecessary pressure on yourself. Give haircuts at your leisure and have fun with them.

Another thing to keep in mind is that you can always snip off more hair, but, once cut, you cannot put it back on. So go easy with the amount of hair you snip away, especially during your first attempt. It's important for you to get a feel for what you're doing, and before you know it, you will be cutting and styling like a pro!

My advice to you is to read through this book carefully and know what you want to do before you do it. Take your time and don't get discouraged (speed and good results will come with experience). And remember, you can always cut off more hair; but, once hair is cut, you cannot put it back on. So take it slow, good luck, and have fun!

1. Haircutting Tools

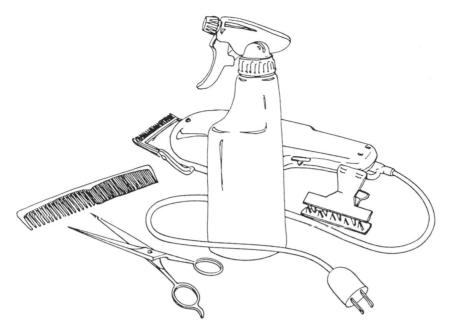

This chapter includes descriptions of various haircutting tools and implements. It is not necessary for you to have all of the items mentioned in order to give a good haircut, but most are suggested to make your task easier. The two tools that are absolutely necessary, however, are a good pair of shears and a haircutting comb. Other items such as spray bottles, hair clips, and capes are useful but not required. For example, hair clips can be helpful especially when cutting long hair. These clips hold sections of hair away from each other, allowing you to work on one section at a time. You may, however, choose not to use clips and simply brush the hair up and twist it back and away from the area. The choice is yours. Other items such as hair clippers are needed only when giving a boy's buzz cut (Chapter 12).

Using the right tools is important. The wrong ones will make your task difficult. A mechanic wouldn't use a trash-bag tie to fasten a hose to a car's engine for obvious reasons. It's the same when using the correct tools for cutting hair. The reasons will become more apparent to you as you read on, and even more obvious when you actually give haircuts. I cannot emphasize enough the benefits of using the appropriate tools.

HAIRCUTTING SHEARS

Shears is another name for scissors, of which there are many different types. Some shears are made for cutting hair, while others are made for use in the garden or the kitchen. Shears can be found in toolboxes, sewing kits, and manicure sets. The shears we are interested in are specifically for cutting hair.

Figure 1.1
Haircutting Shears

A proper pair of shears is your most effective haircutting tool. You can recognize them by their sleekness (Figure 1.1). These scissors are designed for easy use in small places like the area around the ear, which is why they come to a slight point at the end. If you are concerned with using pointed shears on your child's hair, opt for ones with a slightly rounded end. Some shears come with a "pinkie rest" on the end of one of the finger holes. This option is designed to give you better control while cutting. As a beginner, you will probably find this option helpful.

If you are like most people, before you run out and buy a new pair of scissors for giving that first haircut, you will probably want to use a pair that you have around the house. Just make sure that the shears are sharp enough to cut a straight line. You can test scissors for sharpness by taking a piece of thread and doubling it up. Open the scissors and, using gentle pressure, run the doubled thread over one of the blades. The thread should separate easily. Then try this test with the other blade. If your scissors pass the sharpness test, you can probably use them for a tryout haircut.

When shopping for shears, look for a pair that is no longer than five-and-a-half inches. Shears this size are easier to use than larger ones because they won't get in the way of the hair or your hands. Make sure the scissors are comfortable to hold and easy to open and close. You shouldn't have to use pressure in order to close them. The best shears are made of pure steel and have extremely sharp edges. Of course, no matter what the quality of your scissors, never leave them within a child's reach.

You can buy haircutting shears at department stores, cutlery shops, or beauty supply stores. (Most beauty supply stores are open to the general public.) The price of shears can range from under five dollars to over five hundred! Expensive shears for cutting hair are not necessary. A proper inexpensive pair are adequate.

The correct way to hold shears is with your thumb and ring finger. The reason for using your ring finger rather than the middle finger is because it gives more even distribution of pressure on the blades this way. When there is an even balance on the shears, it is easier to cut hair in a straight line.

Depending on the style of the haircut, there are two basic positions for holding the scissors. When cutting a straight line across the bottom of the hair—whether in the back of the head or on the sides—put your thumb and ring finger in the scissor's finger holes. As you cut, hold the scissors horizontally with your thumb and fingertips pointing toward the ground (Figure 1.2a). You will find this position most comfortable.

The second position for holding shears is used when you layer hair. Put your thumb and ring finger in each of the finger holes. Point the tips of the shears toward the ceiling or ground, and keep your fingers pointed toward the head as you cut the hair (see Figure 1.2b).

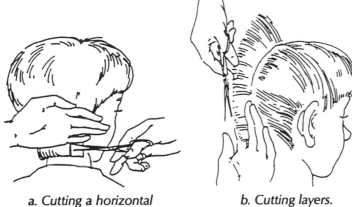

a. Cutting a horizontal straight line.

b. Cutting layers.

Figure 1.2   Proper Scissor-Holding Positions

Your shears will perform best if they are kept clean. After each use, be sure to wipe them off with a dry cloth. You may want to have them sharpened after a period of time. Don't use your shears for anything other than cutting hair. Using them to cut paper even once can noticeably dull the blades.

Another way to care for your shears is to make sure they are tight enough (they can become loose). Check to see if your scissors need tightening by holding one of the finger holes with one hand. Turn the shears on their side with the other finger hole on top. Open up the shears with your free hand, then allow the blades to close by themselves. If they slam closed quickly and completely, they need to be tightened. All you have to do is tighten the screw head that holds the blades together. Tighten them to the point where they nearly close completely.

Remember, you don't have to spend a fortune for a good pair of haircutting scissors. What is important is that they are the right size and sharp enough.

HAIRCUTTING COMB

Everybody knows what a comb is, but do you know what makes a haircutting comb different from others? One side of the comb has fine, closely spaced teeth while the other side has teeth that are thicker and spaced farther apart. The notion behind the design of this comb is really quite logical. When you comb wet hair with a fine-toothed comb, you are actually stretching the hair on the top layer down to the length of the hair underneath. If you cut hair after combing it this way, you will have one length with no graduation of lengths whatsoever. On the other hand, when you use the wider-spaced teeth of the comb, the top layer of hair will be less stressed and will fall a bit longer than the hair combed with the fine teeth. This wider-spaced side of the comb is great to use for one-length haircuts. When you cut your child's hair, make sure your comb gets through the hair easily. You don't want to pull or stretch the hair, you want only an even tension.

The ideal haircutting comb is seven inches long and one inch wide (Figure 1.3). It is all right to use a shorter comb, but the size just mentioned is the easiest to manipulate. A professional haircutting comb, with its fine teeth on one end and wider-spaced teeth on the other, is your best bet. The side you use depends on how thick your child's hair is. As mentioned before, the comb should grab the hair but not pull it.

You can purchase combs almost anywhere. However, professional haircutting combs, which are inexpensive (under three dollars a dozen), are found in beauty supply stores. If you purchase combs elsewhere, just be sure they are the right type.

You probably have plenty of combs around your house that may be suitable to use when you cut hair. Just remember to take

**Figure 1.3
Haircutting Comb**

the comb's size, shape, and the space between its teeth into consideration. You don't want to use a comb that doesn't grab the hair effectively, nor do you want one that is awkward to use. When cutting hair, you are going to have more important things to think about than what to do with your comb.

Most of the time, you should hold the comb with your writing hand, thumb on the bottom and four fingers on top (Figure 1.4). You may want to change this position when you section hair, in which case you would hold the comb as you would a piece of chalk. Any other comb-holding positions are described in the specific haircuts found in this book.

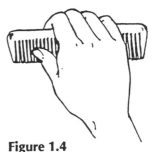

When cutting hair, you can hold both the shears and comb in the same hand. If you hold the shears with your ring finger only, you can flip the shears in and out of the palm of your hand to free up your thumb for combing. When you cut the hair, rest the comb between your thumb and palm.

Figure 1.4 Basic Comb-Holding Position

CAPE

I'll bet you didn't realize that the thing you wear over your clothes during a haircut is called a cape. Well, that's what it is, and it is nothing more than a rectangular piece of plastic or water-resistant material with a hole in it for the neck. The cape's main objective is to keep prickly hair clippings from sticking to clothing and making their way down the neck and back. Although it is not imperative, a cape is certainly a good idea. Without one, your child will become uncomfortable and uneasy.

When shopping for a cape, look for one that is child-size (Figure 1.5). If the cape is too big, your child may not want to wear it. Child-size capes often come with designs that appeal to children.

You can purchase capes in beauty supply stores or through many shop-at-home catalogs. Plastic child-size capes sell for under five dollars.

Capes are also very easy to make, especially if you do any kind of sewing. If you decide to make one, choose water-resistant material, and use snaps or velcro as the fastener. You can also improvise and make a cape by wrapping a large towel or sheet around your child and fastening it at the neck. Be careful not to create too much bulk around the neck; keep the cape as smooth as possible. Simply pin it in the back with a safety pin to keep it snug.

Figure 1.5 Cape

When you put a cape on your child, be sure to take his or her hands out on either side. Kids don't like to be so restricted that they can't use their hands. Also, don't fasten the cape too tightly around the neck. The more comfortable the child, the more cooperative he or she will be during the haircut.

SPRAY BOTTLE

A spray bottle filled with water, simple as it is, can be an extremely useful tool when cutting your child's hair. Not only does it serve to wet the hair, it can entertain your child as well. I have shown my children how to squirt the water from the bottle into their mouths. This usually keeps them occupied long enough for me to cut their hair. I don't let them play with the spray bottle at any other time, only during haircuts. Another thing young children find entertaining is the idea of the water from the spray bottle "raining" on them as you wet their hair. The talk of rain seems to take their mind off the haircut.

You can buy spray bottles almost anywhere. Your local drug store probably sells them for around one dollar. Available in a wide variety of colors, the best spray bottle to use is one that holds about eight ounces of water (Figure 1.6). This size bottle is large enough to hold all the water you need, yet small enough for a young child to be able to play with.

**Figure 1.6
Spray Bottle**

If your child's hair is clean, you need only to fill the bottle with fresh water, spray the hair, then comb through it. The hair should be damp, not dripping wet. If you let your child drink the water, be sure to keep the spray bottle clean. And keep the bottle out of sight, so it will be a special treat at haircutting time.

HAIR CLIPS

Hair clips come in different shapes and sizes. They're suggested to help you keep the hair you are not cutting clipped up and out of your way. Many illustrations in this book show these clips holding sections of hair. Using them will make your task easier, but if you choose not to use clips, simply twist the hair up and away from the area you are working on.

Figure 1.7 shows the type of clip I feel is best to use when cutting hair. Unlike bobby pins, these clips are able to grab a lot of hair and they won't slip. The length and thickness of your child's hair will determine the size clips that are best.

In addition to being helpful while giving a cut, hair clips can also entertain your child. Most children enjoy playing with them, often imagining that they are some kind of creatures because of their teeth. I call them crocodile clips.

You can purchase hair clips at beauty supply and drug stores. They are inexpensive at about two dollars a dozen. As they come in different colors and sizes, they can also be fun to use as decorations in your daughter's hair.

Figure 1.7 Hair Clips

HAIR CLIPPERS

Hair clippers, which are easy to use, cut hair very short and even. You will need to purchase hair clippers only if you are going to be giving a boy's buzz cut (Chapter 12).

Most hair clippers come as part of a set that also includes a large comb, four attachments, a cleaning brush, and oil for the clipper blades (Figure 1.8). The basic clipper attachments cut hair in the following lengths:

Attachment Number	Approximate Hair Length
1	1/4 inch
2	1/2 inch
3	3/4 inch
4	1 inch

Some sets come with additional attachments and/or a pair of scissors. I don't suggest purchasing this type of set as the scissors are usually too long and not worth the additional cost. Buy good-quality essentials only, not the unnecessary extras.

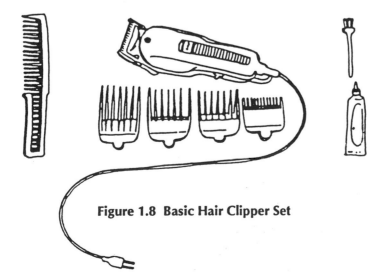

Figure 1.8 Basic Hair Clipper Set

You can buy clippers at most drug, department, and beauty supply stores. They range in price from about fifteen to forty dollars. Your clippers will serve you best if you follow the manufacturer's care instructions. Be sure to oil the blades to keep them from rusting and to prevent them from sticking.

2. General Information and Helpful Hints

This chapter includes a potpourri of information that you will find helpful in your quest to beautify your child's hair. Included are tips on how to determine the best hairstyle for your child, the best kinds of shampoos to use, and how to handle some common haircutting problems. Safety precautions are also presented.

SAFETY

First and foremost—be careful! Undoubtedly, your child will move during the haircut. Most times, especially with babies and very young children, I find myself doing more dodging than haircutting. Razor-sharp shears can easily cut your child's ear or your own hand, so be prepared to move with your child as you trim and cut. As mentioned in Chapter 1, good-quality scissors with rounded ends are available. You might feel more comfortable working with this type of shears. No matter what the cutting tool, the most important thing is to be aware that your child, undoubtedly, will fidget during the haircut.

Watch where you leave your scissors when you put them down. It takes only a moment for a child to grab them. Aside from the obvious dangers, you don't want to see your child giving a surprise haircut to himself or a sibling.

THE BEST HAIRSTYLE FOR YOUR CHILD

**Figure 2.1
Boy's Wedge Cut**

Everyone's hair is different—curly, straight, thick, thin, coarse, fine, or wavy. The terms thick and thin refer to the amount of hair on the head. Someone with a lot of hair has thick hair, while those with thin hair have little. Coarse and fine are words that describe texture. Coarse hair is hard to handle, resistant to curl, and generally wiry like steel wool. Fine hair is soft and flyaway. Most babies have fine hair, which usually changes with age. The words curly, straight, and wavy describe the amount of bend in the hair.

If your child's hair is thin and/or fine, you should probably keep it one length. In a one-length haircut, all the hair ends at the same bottom line. This style allows hair to look its fullest and appear thicker than it actually is. For boys, the wedge cut (Figure 2.1) described in Chapter 10 is the best choice. For girls, the one-length cut (Figure 2.2) presented in Chapter 6 is best.

If your child's hair is thick and/or coarse, layering is often the best way to tame it. When you layer hair, you cut and shape it much the same way you trim a bush. The shape of the haircut can be anything you want once you understand basic layering techniques. For boys, follow the layered cut instructions in Chapter 11. If you prefer a shorter version, the buzz cut in Chapter 12 is a good choice. For girls, choose the basic layered haircut in Chapter 8, or the angled cut found in Chapter 7. If you really want your daughter to have a one-length haircut, but she has very thick hair, be sure to keep it short, shoulder-length at the longest. Thick hair tends to be difficult to comb out when it gets long.

**Figure 2.2
Girl's One-Length Cut**

If your child has very straight hair, to the point that it sticks out everywhere, it is best to leave some length on the top. The weight of a heavy top layer will help keep the hair under control. One-length haircuts are good options here. Styling aids are also helpful. Applying a little styling gel to wet hair will help the hair to keep its shape once combed.

Curly hair looks good in a variety of shapes and lengths. While it is hard to determine the best style for your child, in my opinion, layers are usually the best bet. Some curly hair, no matter how long and heavy it is, will always look "big." This is when layering is the best choice. With layers, you can give the hair shape. Hair that is less curly or wavy is okay for almost any style. When cutting curly hair, pull it out straight, then cut it the same way you would straight hair. You must be careful, however, for curly hair (more than any other type) shrinks when it dries. The curlier the hair, the more it will shrink. So be careful.

SNARLED HAIR

A common problem, especially for little girls, is snarled, tangled hair. Many children don't like to have their hair brushed. (Often, it's enough of a job just getting them dressed in the morning.) When a brush doesn't go through the hair easily, it can be very painful for your child. At one time, an electic comb for removing tangles was available. Good idea, but not very effective.

There are several factors that can account for snarled hair. Most frequently, hair that is long and not brushed often enough gets snarled. The longer the hair, the more brushing it needs. If you are like most busy parents, you probably don't spend a lot of time brushing your child's hair. Cutting the hair to a shorter length is one solution. You can also teach your child to brush his or her own hair, and encourage brushing twice a day, once in the morning and once before bed.

Dry, damaged hair can also be difficult to brush. Hair can become damaged from exposure to such things as the sun and wind. If hair is not trimmed regularly, the ends will get dry. If this is a problem with your child's hair, you'll need to condition it. After washing the hair, apply a small amount of conditioner to the ends and comb it through. Leave the conditioner in a minute or two before rinsing it out. The conditioning may be all that your child's hair needs at the time, but the ends should eventually be trimmed. Trimming the ends every six to eight weeks is suggested to avoid dry ends.

Children who repeatedly swim in chlorinated water acquire a build-up of chlorine in their hair. This causes the hair to become dry and feel like cotton candy. Chemicals in your household water can also cause hair to feel funny or result in such problems as turning blonde hair green. Drug and beauty supply stores sell clarifying or dechlorinating shampoos for treating this specific problem.

COWLICS

I think everybody knows someone who has a cowlick. A cowlick is a section of hair, usually near the hairline, that grows in a different direction from the rest. This tuft of hair sticks up and refuses to lie down flat (Figure 2.3).

In my opinion, cowlicks add to a person's character. I think they look very cute on little kids. Most people who have cowlicks, however, do not share my opinion. If your child has a cowlick, there are some things you might be able to do to make it less obvious.

The best way to handle this stubborn patch of hair, is to keep the hair heavy in that area and try to maintain a style that goes with the cowlick. For example, let's say that your son has a cowlick on the left side of his forehead. Try parting his hair on the left and combing it back. Also, when you cut his hair, leave the cowlic area slightly longer than the rest. It may look uneven when wet, but when it dries, the cowlick will shrink up and blend with the rest of the hair.

**Figure 2.3
Cowlick at
the Hairline**

SHAMPOOS

The shampoo you use can make a difference in the health and manageability of your child's hair (and yours, too, for that matter). The natural pH level of hair is between 4.5 and 5.5. If you use a shampoo that has a much higher pH level, the result will likely be damaged hair. Chemicals found in hair colorants and permanent solutions have extreme pH factors to penetrate the outer layer of the hair. Watch out. Some shampoos found on the market have, in fact, the same pH level as some of these chemicals.

When you shop for shampoo, look for one that has a low pH level. Many shampoo manufacturers identify the pH levels of their products. The best level is between 3 and 7. Read labels carefully.

SOME GENERAL SUGGESTIONS

Keep the following points in mind while giving your child a haircut. These suggestions are designed to help you achieve positive haircutting results.

Follow the Sectioning System

The sectioning system that I have mapped out in detail in Chapter 3, is designed to help you keep track of the areas of hair that you have and haven't cut. Sectioning hair also allows you to cut one area, while the remaining sections are clipped up and out of your way.

Each time you give a complete haircut, be sure to cut the sections in the proper order. By order, I mean start with the back sections first (Sections 1 and 2), then move to the right side (Section 3), and finish up with the left side (Section 4). Cutting the sections in order will prevent you from "getting lost" in your haircut.

Talk to Your Child

It always helps to talk to your child while cutting his or her hair. Since you are going to be together, and your child has little to do, why not take advantage of this opportunity to communicate with and get to know your child better? Discuss such subjects as school, favorite toys and games, or friends.

I find, most of the time, I have to ask a lot of questions to get a conversation going, especially with preschoolers. My attempts usually elicit smiles and lots of conversation. For best results, discuss positive things and keep the discussion light.

3. Sectioning Hair

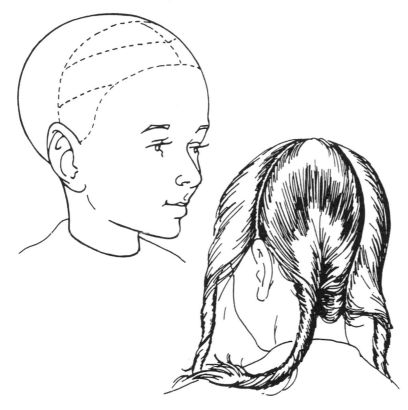

Sectioning is a term that describes parting the hair prior to giving a haircut. You divide the hair into different sections in order to isolate the hair you need to cut. Most times, when giving a complete haircut, you will be using four basic sections. Other times, such as when you give a partial haircut, you may need only two of the basic sections. For extremely thick or long hair, these basic sections may need to be further divided into subsections.

Before going on, please refer to Figure 3.1 to familiarize yourself with some common terms used throughout this and other chapters of the book.

THE FOUR BASIC SECTIONS

In order to separate hair into the four basic sections, simply follow the steps on the next page. To section properly, always start with damp hair.

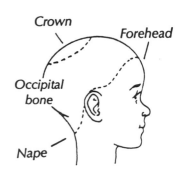

Figure 3.1
Areas of the Head

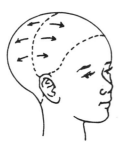

1 First, you must separate the front section from the back. Using the end of your comb as you would a drawing tool, make a line on the scalp from the crown of the head to the highest point of the hairline above each ear. Comb this hair forward, separating it from the hair in the back.

*Separate the front section
from the back.*

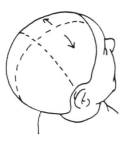

2 Drawing a line with your comb, divide this front section in half, separating the right and left sides. Twist or clip up each of these sections, making sure you can see the scalp lines.

*Separate the right and left sides
of the front section.*

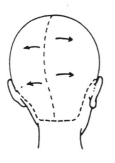

3 Next, divide the back section in half by drawing a line with your comb down the center of the back of the head. As you did with the side sections, keep the back sections separated by twisting or clipping them up and out of the way.

*Separate the right and left sides
of the back section.*

Figure 3.2 on the next page shows the four basic sections. Notice how the sections are numbered. If you get in the habit of cutting the sections in their numbered order, it will be easy for you to keep track of what you have and have not cut.

Always try to begin cutting hair in the back section, but if your child is young and will not sit still for very long, you may choose to cut the two side sections first and save the back for another day.

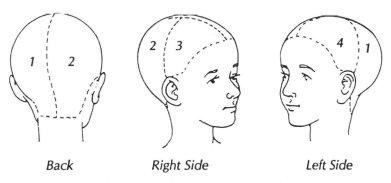

Back   *Right Side*   *Left Side*

Figure 3.2 The Four Basic Sections

SUBSECTIONS

Thick or layered hair is easier to cut if you divide the basic sections further. Also, certain haircuts, such as the layered cut, require subsections. A basic section can be subdivided vertically, horizontally, or diagonally (Figure 3.3).

Subsections are made in the same way as the basic sections. For instance, if you wish to subdivide a basic section horizontally, draw a horizontal line with your comb across the section. Let down the hair below the line (you will be working on this hair first), while twisting away or clipping up the hair above the line.

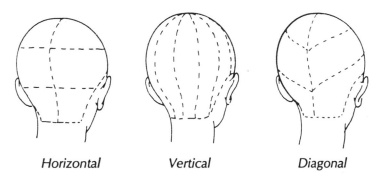

Horizontal   *Vertical*   *Diagonal*

Figure 3.3 Subsections

A FINAL WORD ABOUT SECTIONING

Although sectioning hair may seem to be an unnecessary step, be assured that it is quite critical to a successful haircut. Do not skip this step! Taking a few minutes to organize the hair into sections (or subsections) will save you time in the long run.

4. Cutting Baby's Hair

When you have a new baby, you probably won't give much thought to styling his or her hair. After all, there usually isn't much to work with, especially in the beginning. That first hair is in a once-in-a-lifetime form. Know that those precious baby curls, once cut, will probably be gone forever, so enjoy them as long as possible. However, when that day comes when your son's hair is hanging in his eyes, or the bottom of your daughter's hair looks pretty ragged, you will know that the time has come for that inevitable first haircut. The next question is whether a trip to the barber or hairstylist is really necessary. I don't think so. With a little guidance, I am betting that you can cut your child's hair yourself.

The age when a child needs that first haircut varies with each child. Some are born with a lot of hair, while others are completely bald. Whatever the case, when your child is ready for a trim, you'll know it. In my experience, the average age for a child's first haircut is around one year. As you know, a child that age won't have any idea what you are trying to do when you give the haircut. Children that age do understand, however, a lot more than you think. And it's a good idea to at least try to prepare them for the upcoming event.

Prior to that first haircut, try to explain to your child what you are going to do. Give some information on what he or she should expect. As ridiculous as this may seem, talking to a one-year-old is far from pointless. After all, we constantly talk to our pets, and they couldn't possibly understand half of what your child can. In preparation for the actual event, read a children's book about getting a haircut to your child.

Try to make the haircut sound exciting and special. Make your child feel like this is something he or she wants. Of course, every child is different, so this preparation tactic may be effective for some but not for all. If your child reacts in a positive way, give the haircut as soon as possible—that day or the next—while the idea is still appealing. While giving the haircut, constantly assure the child that the experience is fun and painless. Give lots of praise for good behavior.

If your child is afraid of the scissors or is tough and uncooperative about getting a haircut, you may have to be a little sneaky about the whole thing. Try to divert your child's attention by giving the haircut during bathtime or while he or she is playing with a toy. Keep the scissors hidden as best you can. If your child catches you after you've snipped a lock or two, say something like, "See that, you didn't feel a thing!" Continue to assure and convince the child that haircuts are good things. If you still have no luck, it might be best not to bring up the subject again for a few weeks or months. What you can do, however, is try to cut your child's hair during naptime (at least the bangs).

Brushing baby's hair every day will make him or her comfortable with this act. Habits are formed during the early stages in life. The older a child gets, the more difficult it will become to change routines. If you are not in the habit of brushing your baby's hair, start now. By the time your baby is three years old, he or she will probably want to brush his or her own hair. It's never too early to start good grooming habits.

Another word of advice when cutting baby's hair—keep the hairstyle simple. Stay away from involved layered cuts. Your main objective should be to keep your young child looking neat. Usually this can be achieved by cutting just the hair that is out of place. For instance, if the bangs are too long, but the rest of the hair looks fine, cut the bangs only.

INSTRUCTIONS FOR CUTTING BABY'S HAIR

Tools: Shears, • comb, • spray bottle of water (optional)

1 First, dampen the baby's hair. Next, comb down the dampened hair where it needs cutting, and hold a section of this hair between your forefinger and middle finger.

Comb the hair between your fingers.

2 Slide your fingers (with the hair between them) to the desired length; quickly and carefully cut the hair.

Cut the hair.

When Cutting Baby's Hair . . .

If you have difficulty getting your baby to sit still for a haircut, try one or more of the following suggestions:

- *Sit the child in a high chair with his or her favorite toy.*
- *Have another adult hold your child while you cut the hair.*
- *Situate yourselves in front of a mirror. This way the child can see what you are doing. Boys especially are anxious when you cut around their ears, so watching as you snip might make your child more comfortable.*

Cut your baby's hair wherever and whenever you can. Anything goes when dealing with baby. Know that most people find it difficult to cut a baby's hair. You, however, have an advantage since the child is yours and you know best how to handle him or her.

Home is probably the best place to give your baby a haircut. Familiar surroundings usually create a comfortable atmosphere.

Young boys generally need more attention than girls when it comes to cutting hair. Try to trim around your son's ears and cut his bangs until he is around two years of age. At that time he will probably be ready for one of the haircuts detailed in this book.

Be firm with your child when it's time for his or her first haircut, just as you are about trimming fingernails, brushing teeth, and any other necessary task. After a haircut, be sure to point out how pretty or handsome he or she looks. Encourage other family members to express positive comments, also. Children love praise and attention, so don't be surprised if, after using these flattery techniques a few times, they actually start asking for haircuts.

When you feel the time has come for your child's first haircut, keep the following tips in mind:

- Know the hairstyle you want your child have.
- Look over the instructions for that haircut before you do any cutting.
- Know that it isn't necessary to follow the instructions exactly as they are presented. Children under three years old usually won't sit still long enough for you to do each and every step.
- First cut that part of the hair that needs to be trimmed the most. In case your child can stand no more, at least that part will be done.
- Be careful not to cut your child or yourself. Be prepared to move your hands along with the movement of your child's head as he or she fidgets.

In addition to the suggestions just given, remember to be confident and enjoy what you are doing. Your positive attitude will rub off on your child.

5. Cutting Bangs

Bangs can be worn, in one variation or another, with just about every haircut. They can be layered or blunt, and as thick or thin as you like. Bangs are such a small part of your hairstyle, but they make the most difference in the way you look. One cannot help but notice when someone's bangs are too short, too long, or just plain crooked!

Parents often cut their children's bangs themselves, but are seldom really happy with the results. I can always remember Dad's home haircuts by simply looking at my elementary school pictures. There were those ever-crooked bangs! I always wondered what was so difficult about cutting a straight line. With experience, I discovered the key to making bangs look good. First, you must section the hair properly, then you must cut the bangs in three steps.

When cutting your child's bangs, you'll need to dampen the bang area only, not the entire head. If your child is small, sit him or her up on a table rather than a chair. This might make it easier for you to see exactly where the bangs reach. You may want to get the rest of your child's hair out of the way by using hair clips or putting it up in a ponytail.

When cutting bangs on a boy, it is usually a good idea to make as wide a bang section as possible to better blend with the rest of his hair. In general, it is not a good idea to cut only the bangs on a boy (as opposed to a full haircut) unless you need a "quick fix." If you continually cut only the bangs, it won't be long before he begins to look like a she!

INSTRUCTIONS FOR CUTTING BASIC BANGS

Tools: Shears, • comb, • spray bottle of water (optional), • cape (optional), • hair clips (optional)

1 Using the spray bottle, wet the front of the hair. Section off a pie-shaped area of bangs by making a line from the top of the crown to the outermost point of each eyebrow with your comb. Check to make sure both sides look even before going on.

Section the bang area.

2 Comb down the hair in the center of the bang area. Slide your forefinger and middle finger around this center section of hair and pull it down to the desired bang length.

Hold the center section of bangs at the desired length.

3 Using your middle finger as a guide, cut the hair in a straight line. As you cut, be careful not to lift the hair. Keep your fingers against the child's head. (Cutting hair that has been lifted from the head will result in layers.)

The best length for bangs is at the eyebrows. And remember, wet hair "shrinks" when it dries, so cut the bangs slightly below or exactly at the eyebrows.

Cut the center section of bangs.

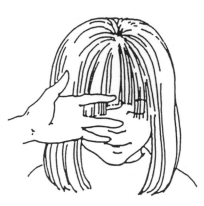

4 Comb the hair on the left side of the bang section together with some of the hair you have just cut from the center section. As before, slide your two fingers around this hair, pull it down, and cut the hair to match the center section. Comb the cut hair and let it fall naturally to make sure is looks straight. If not, repeat Steps 2 and 3 and remove any uneven ends.

Cut one side of the bang section.

5 Now comb the hair on the right side of the bang section. Place this hair between your two fingers along with some of the cut hair. As before, cut the hair straight to match the rest. Comb the hair again and let it fall naturally.

Cut the remaining hair in the bang section.

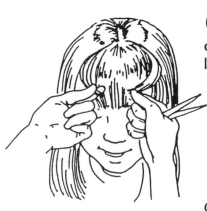

6 To check the bangs for evenness, pull a piece of hair from each end and compare them in the center of the forehead. If they are not even, trim a little hair from the longer side.

Check the bangs for evenness.

Congratulations! You have just cut your child's bangs and they are straight and neat.

Variation

If you want to layer the bangs, comb the entire bang section up and cut off the top inch or so. This will leave the bangs with a thinned-out effect. You can blow-dry the bangs back to make them look fluffy and full. I don't recommend this type of bang for girls with thin hair unless you want the bangs to look wispy.

Layer the bangs.

6. Girl's One-Length Haircut

The one-length haircut is the all-time favorite for most parents. It looks neat, is easy to maintain, and can be worn in many different ways. This haircut is good for any hair type. However, if your child has very curly hair, this style will look best at a short, above-the-shoulder length. The one-length cut is easy to maintain. Simply brush it and leave it as is, or put in up in a ponytail or braid. (See Chapter 9 for styling tips and ideas.) Here's the best part—this cut is easy to give. All of the hair ends meet at the longest length; there are no layers.

The hair should be clean and damp prior to cutting. If the hair is already clean, either spray it with water from your spray bottle or wet it in the sink or tub. Keep the hair damp during the haircut. If the section of hair you are working on gets dry, simply spray it with a little water.

Your work area should be in a room with a hard floor. Hair clippings are easier to sweep up than they are to vacuum. In most cases, the kitchen is the ideal spot.

Two sets of instructions are presented for the one-length haircut. One set is for children who have thin hair or who are under five years old. A separate set of instructions, beginning on page 35, is for children with thick hair.

ONE-LENGTH HAIRCUT INSTRUCTIONS FOR THIN HAIR

Tools: Shears, • comb, • spray bottle of water (optional), • cape (optional), • hair clips (optional)

1 Divide the hair into the four basic sections, described in detail beginning on page 16. You may choose to clip up the sections or twist them away from each other.

The four basic sections.

2 Let down the hair in Sections 1 and 2 (the back sections). Comb the hair down straight.

Comb down the hair in the back sections.

3 Have your child sit up straight and tilt her head forward, chin down.

Tilt the head forward.

Comb the hair in the center of the back section straight down. Slip your forefinger and middle finger around the hair you are combing.

Slip your fingers around the hair.

5 Slide the two fingers, with the hair between them, down to the desired length.

Hold the section of hair at the desired length.

6 Holding the shears horizontally with your finger-tips pointing toward the ground, cut the hair between your two fingers. As you cut, be careful not to lift up the hair. (Cutting hair that has been lifted from the head will result in layers.)

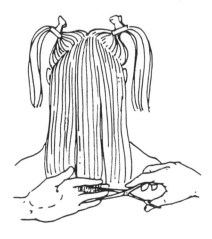

Cut the hair straight across.

7 Combine the remaining hair on the left side with some of the hair you have just cut. Holding this hair between your two fingers, and using your first cut as a guide, cut the hair in a straight line.

Combine the remaining hair on the left side with some of the cut hair.

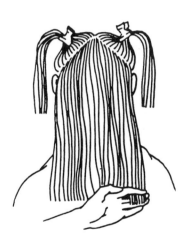

8 To complete the straight line across the back section, combine the remaining hair on the right side with some of the cut hair. Holding this hair between your two fingers, and using the cut hair as a guide, cut the hair in a straight line.

Combine the remaining hair on the right side with some of the cut hair.

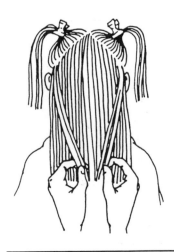

9 Check to make sure the hair length in the back section is even by pulling a little hair from each end toward the center. Do not elevate the hair. If the hair lengths do not match, trim small amounts of hair where needed to even them out, using your center cut as a guide.

Check for evenness.

10 The back section is now complete.

Completed back section.

11 Next, you will be cutting the sides of the hair to match the back. Let down the hair in Section 3 and comb it straight down. Have your child look straight ahead with her shoulders relaxed.

Comb the hair in Section 3.

12 Including some hair from the back section to use as a cutting guide, comb the hair in Section 3 between your two fingers. Slide your fingers down to meet the new hair length. Cut the hair straight across to meet your guide.

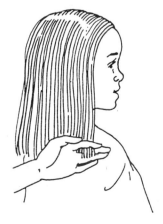

Combine the hair in Section 3 with some hair from the back section.

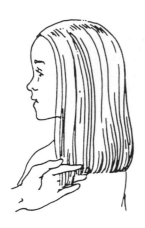

13 Next, let down the hair in Section 4. Including some hair from the back section to use as a cutting guide, comb the hair in Section 4 between your two fingers. Slide your fingers down to meet the new hair length. Cut the hair straight across to meet your guide.

*Combine the hair in Section 4
with some hair from the back section.*

14 To check for evenness, pull both side sections together and match them under the chin. If one side seems longer, trim away a small amount of hair from that side.

Check the sides for evenness.

Congratulations! You have just completed the one-length haircut for thin hair.

ONE-LENGTH HAIRCUT INSTRUCTIONS FOR THICK HAIR

Tools: Shears, • comb, • spray bottle of water (optional), • cape (optional), • hair clips (optional)

1 Divide the hair into the four basic sections, described in detail beginning on page 16. You may choose to clip up the sections or twist them away from each other.

The four basic sections

2 Let down the hair in Section 1. Using your comb, make a horizontal subsection about halfway down this section. (For detailed information on subsections, refer to page 17.) Clip up the hair on top and let the hair at the bottom hang down (you will be working on this hair first). As you have just done, make a horizontal subsection with the hair in Section 2.

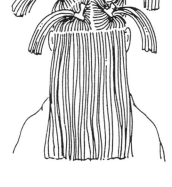

Separate the back into horizontal subsections.

3 Have your child sit up straight and tilt her head forward, chin down.

Tilt the head forward.

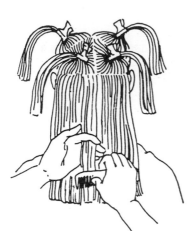

4 Comb the hair in the center of the back section straight down. Slip your forefinger and middle finger around the hair you are combing.

Slip your fingers around the hair.

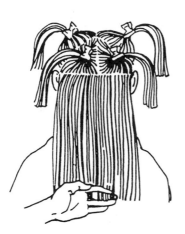

5 Slide the two fingers, with the hair between them, down to the desired length.

Hold the section of hair at the desired length.

6 Holding the shears horizontally with your fingertips pointing toward the ground, cut the hair between your two fingers. As you cut, be careful not to lift up the hair. (Cutting hair that has been lifted from the head will result in layers.)

Cut the hair straight across.

7 Combine the remaining hair on the left side with some of the hair you have just cut. Holding this hair between your two fingers, and using your first cut as a guide, cut the hair in a straight line.

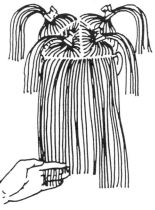

Combine the remaining hair on the left side with some of the cut hair.

8 To complete the straight line across the back section, combine the remaining hair on the right side with some of the cut hair. Holding this hair between your two fingers, and using the cut hair as a guide, cut the hair in a straight line.

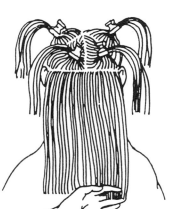

Combine the remaining hair on the right side with some of the cut hair.

9 Check to make sure the hair length in the back section is even by pulling a little hair from each end toward the center. Do not elevate the hair. If the hair lengths do not match, trim small amounts of hair where needed to even them out, using your center cut as a guide.

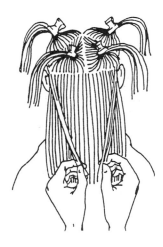

Check for evenness.
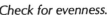

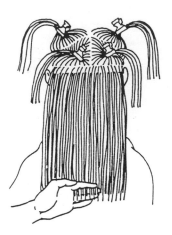

10 Now that you have cut a straight line across the bottom subsections, you will be using this line as a cutting guide for the remaining subsections. Take the hair that is clipped up in Section 1 and divide it in half horizontally. Clip up the hair on top and let the hair at the bottom hang down. Do the same with the hair in Section 2. The hair that is hanging will be longer than the hair you have just cut.

Further divide the back into subsections.

11 Comb the center of the hair between your two fingers and cut the hair to match the guide, but do not cut the guide itself. Cut the remaining hair in this subsection.

Cut the hair in the next subsection.

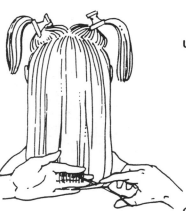

12 Let down the rest of the hair that is clipped up in Sections 1 and 2. As you did before, use the cut hair as a guide and cut this remaining hair.

Cut the remaining hair in the back section.

13 Check the hair lengths for evenness as you did in Step 9. The entire back section is now complete.

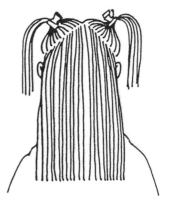

The completed back section.

14 Next, you will be cutting the sides of the hair to match the back. Let down the hair in Section 3 and comb it straight down. Make a horizontal subsection by dividing the hair in half. (If the child's hair is very thick, make three subsections.) Clip up the hair on top and let the hair at the bottom hang down (you will be working on this hair first).

Separate Section 3 into horizontal subsections.

15 Including some hair from the back section to use as a cutting guide, comb the hair in Section 3 between your two fingers. Slide your fingers down to meet the new hair length. Cut the hair straight across to meet your guide.

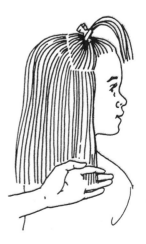

Combine the hair in Section 3 with some hair from the back section.

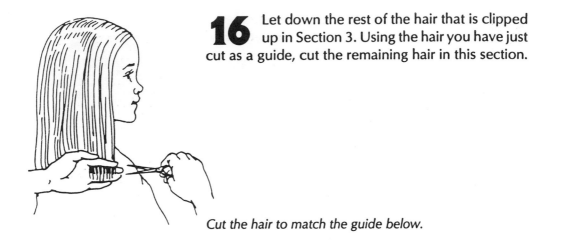

16 Let down the rest of the hair that is clipped up in Section 3. Using the hair you have just cut as a guide, cut the remaining hair in this section.

Cut the hair to match the guide below.

17 As you did with the hair in Section 3, divide the hair in Section 4 into horizontal subsections. Clip up the hair on top and let the hair at the bottom hang down (you will be working on this hair first).

Separate Section 4 into horizontal subsections.

18 Including some of the hair from the back section to use as a cutting guide, comb the hair in Section 4 between your two fingers. Slide your fingers down to meet the new hair length. Cut the hair straight across to meet your guide.

*Combine the hair in Section 4
with some hair from the back section.*

19 Let down the rest of the hair that is clipped up in Section 4. Using the hair you have just cut as a guide, cut the remaining hair in this section.

Cut the hair to match the guide below.

20 Check the sides for evenness by pulling both side sections together and matching them under the chin. If one side seems longer, trim a small amount of hair from that side.

Check the sides for evenness.

Congratulations! You have just completed the one-length haircut for thick hair.

7. Girl's Angled Haircut

The angled haircut, or feathered cut, is great for any hair type. The hair, which graduates in length from the bangs to the longest hair in the back section, frames the face nicely. After washing angle-cut hair, either let it air dry or blow it back to feather the sides.

It is not difficult to give an angled haircut, but if your child has extremely long hair, you must be careful to cut both sides exactly the same. And although this haircut is good for any type of hair, very straight hair can be exceptionally challenging as it shows every imperfection.

The hair should be clean and damp prior to cutting. If the hair is already clean, either spray it with water from your spray bottle or wet it in the sink or tub. Keep the hair damp during the haircut. If the section of hair you are working on gets dry, simply spray it with a little water.

Your work area should be in a room with a hard floor. Hair clippings are easier to sweep up than they are to vacuum. In most cases, the kitchen is the ideal spot.

INSTRUCTIONS FOR GIVING AN ANGLED HAIRCUT

Tools: Shears, • comb, • spray bottle of water (optional), • cape (optional), • hair clips (optional)

1 Divide the hair into the the four basic sections, described in detail beginning on page 16. You may choose to clip up the sections or twist them away from each other.

The four basic sections.

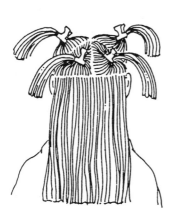

2 Let down the hair in Section 1. Using your comb, make a horizontal subsection about halfway down this section. (For detailed information on subsections, refer to page 17). Clip up the hair on top and let the hair at the bottom hang down (you will be working on this hair first). As you have just done, make a horizontal subsection with the hair in Section 2.

Separate the back into horizontal subsections.

3 Have your child sit up straight and tilt her head forward, chin down.

Tilt the head forward.

4 Comb the hair in the center of the back section straight down. Slip your forefinger and middle finger around the hair you are combing.

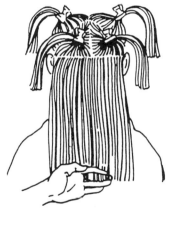

Slip your fingers around the hair.

5 Slide the two fingers, with the hair between them, down to the desired length.

Hold the section of hair at the desired length.

6 Holding the shears horizontally with your finger-tips pointing toward the ground, cut the hair between your two fingers. As you cut, be careful not to lift up the hair. (Cutting hair that has been lifted from the head will result in layers.)

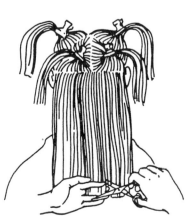

Cut the hair straight across.

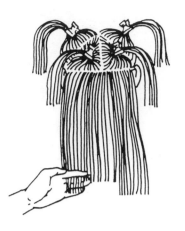

7 Combine the remaining hair on the left side with some of the hair you have just cut. Holding this hair between your two fingers, and using your first cut as a guide, cut the hair in a straight line.

Combine the remaining hair on the left side with some of the cut hair.

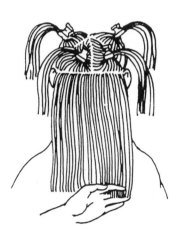

8 To complete the straight line across the back section, combine the remaining hair on the right side with some of the cut hair. Holding this hair between your two fingers, and using the cut hair as a guide, cut the hair in a straight line.

Combine the remaining hair on the right side with some of the cut hair.

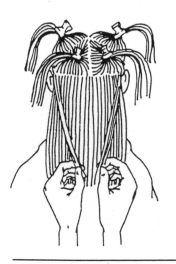

9 Check to make sure the hair length in the back section is even by pulling a little hair from each end toward the center. Do not elevate this hair. If the hair lengths do not match, trim small amounts of hair where needed to even them out, using your center cut as a guide.

Check for evenness.

10 Now that you have cut a straight line across the bottom subsections, you will be using this line as a cutting guide for the remaining subsections. Take the hair that is clipped up in Section 1 and divide it in half horizontally. Clip up the hair in the top half and let the hair at the bottom hang down. Do the same with the hair in Section 2. The hair that is hanging will be longer than the hair you have just cut.

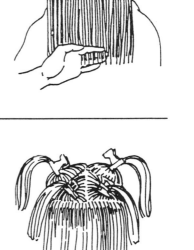

Further divide the back into subsections.

11 Comb the center of the hair between your two fingers and cut the hair to match the guide, but do not cut the guide itself. Use this guide to cut the remaining hair in this section.

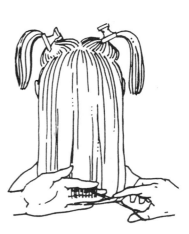

Cut the hair in the next subsection.

12 Let down the rest of the hair that is clipped up in Sections 1 and 2. As you did before, use the cut hair as a guide and cut this remaining hair.

Cut the remaining hair in the back section.

13 Check the hair length for evenness as you did in Step 9. The entire back section is now complete.

The completed back section.

14 Next you will be cutting the sides of the hair. Let down the hair in Section 3 and comb it straight down. Make a diagonal subsection by dividing the hair in half. (If the child's hair is very thick, make two subsections.) Clip up the hair on top and let the hair at the bottom hang down (you will be working with this hair first.)

Divide Section 3 into diagonal subsections.

15 Including some of the hair from the back as your cutting guide, comb the hair in Section 3 between your two fingers. Cut this hair straight across to match the hair from the back. The piece of hair you have just cut will be referred to as your *long-side guide.*

Cut the long-side guide.

16 Next, move to the bangs at the top of this section (bangs from Section 4 can be combined here). Push or clip the back section out of your way. Comb the hair between your two fingers. Holding the hair, slide your fingers down until your middle finger rests in the groove just below the eyebrows. Cut the bangs at this length. This piece of hair will be referred to as your *short-side guide.*

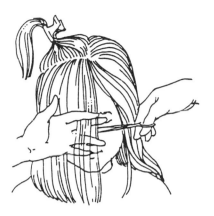

Cut the short-side guide.

17 Now you have established your shortest length, which is at the top of this section, and your longest length, which is at the bottom.

The shortest and longest hair lengths.

18 To bring the two lengths together, you must cut the hair between them at an angle. Comb the hair in Section 3 forward. Push or clip the back section out of your way. Including a piece of hair from the long-side guide, comb the bottom half of this section between your two fingers. Pull this hair forward and angle your fingers so that they are aimed at the short-side guide. Your middle finger should be resting somewhere along the side of the nose and the center of the chin.

Angle your fingers toward the short-side guide.

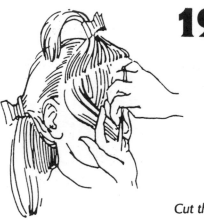

19 Cut the hair between your two fingers to match the long-side guide.

Cut the hair at the bottom half of this section.

20 Next, comb the hair that is in the upper half of Section 3 between your fingers. Include some of the hair from the short-side guide, as well as a piece of the hair you have just cut.

Comb the hair in the upper half of Section 3.

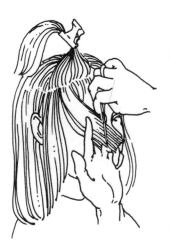

21 With your middle finger resting somewhere along the cheekbone, cut the hair to bring it all together.

Cut the hair.

22 Once you have angle-cut the hair (from the short-side guide to the long-side), unclip the remaining hair in Section 3 and comb it over the hair you have just cut. Using the hair underneath as your guide, cut the remaining hair, but be careful not to cut the guide.

Cut the hair to match the guide.

23 Now move to Section 4. First divide the hair into diagonal subsections, then cut the hair as you did in Section 3 (Steps 14–22).

Cut the hair in Section 4.

24 Once you have cut both sides, check for evenness by combing all of the hair slightly forward. The hair should frame the face evenly. If anything looks off, correct it by going through the steps again.

The completed angle cut.

Congratulations! You have just completed the girl's angled haircut.

8. Girl's Layered Haircut

The layered haircut is the most complex of the girl's cuts presented in this book. You must give the hair around the perimeter of the head an angled cut, as well as cut layers on the top. When layering, the hair on top must be shorter than the hair on the bottom, but all of the hair must blend together to give a third dimension to the cut. (Know that giving this haircut is easier than it sounds.)

This haircut is perfect if your child's hair is very thick or unruly. Extremely curly hair that is uncontrollable is a prime candidate for a layered cut, as is hair with an uneven curl.

Layers can be cut in a number of ways. I have presented the easiest method, which allows the greatest amount of hair length. Whether the hair is blow-dried or air-dried, the layers will give this style more volume than any other cut.

The hair should be clean and damp prior to cutting. If the hair is already clean, either spray it with water from your spray bottle or wet it in the tub or sink. Keep the hair damp during the haircut. If the section of hair you are working on gets dry, simply spray it with a little water.

Your work area should be in a room with a hard floor. Hair clippings are easier to sweep up than they are to vacuum. In most cases, the kitchen is the ideal spot.

INSTRUCTIONS FOR GIVING THE GIRL'S LAYERED HAIRCUT

Tools: Shears, • comb, • spray bottle of water (optional), • cape (optional), • hair clips (optional)

1 Divide the hair into the four basic sections, described in detail beginning on page 16. You may choose to clip up the sections or twist them away from each other.

The four basic sections.

2 Begin with the hair in Section 1. Using your comb, make a diagonal subsection at the top. (For more detailed information on subsections, refer to page 17.) Lift this hair straight up and hold it between your forefinger and middle finger.

Lift up the hair in the top subsection.

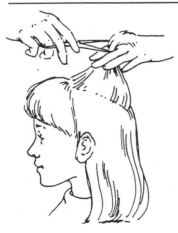

3 Holding the shears with your fingertips pointing toward the head, cut the hair to a length of approximately three inches. You will be using this hair as a cutting guide for the layers in the back section.

Cut the top subsection.

4 If the hair is thick, make the next diagonal subsection about an inch below the one you have just cut. If the hair is thin to medium, work with larger subsections as shown here. Comb the next subsection straight up along with the hair you have just cut (your guide). Cut the hair to match the guide. Make sure your child keeps her head straight, and that you elevate the hair to the same point each time.

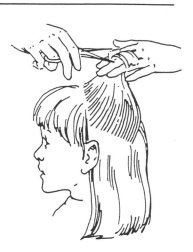

*Comb the next subsection of hair up
and cut it to match the guide.*

5 Continue to work your way down the section, bringing each subsection up and cutting it to match the guide.

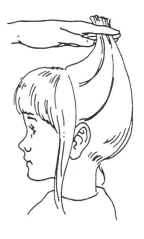

Cut the remaining subsections in Section 1.

6 Once you have layered Section 1, move on to Section 2. (At this point, do not clip or twist the hair in Section 1 out of the way.) When you separate the first diagonal subsection, be sure to add some hair from the top of Section 1 to use as a cutting guide. Holding the hair between your two fingers, cut the hair to match the guide.

*Combine the subsection
with some hair from Section 1.*

7 Once this top subsection is cut, you can comb or clip the hair in Section 1 out of your way. Using this top section of hair as your guide, layer the rest of Section 2 as you did Section 1.

Cut the remaining subsections in Section 2.

8 The entire back section is now layered. Next you must cut this section to the desired length. First comb the hair in the center straight down. Slip your forefinger and middle finger around the hair you are combing.

Slip your fingers around the hair.

9 Slide the two fingers, with the hair between them, to the desired length.

Hold the section of hair at the desired length.

10 Holding the shears horizontally with your fingertips pointing toward the ground, cut the hair between your two fingers. As you cut, be careful not to lift up the hair. (Cutting hair that has been lifted from the head will result in layers.) If the hair is curly, be sure to wet it enough to smooth out the curl. This will allow you to cut a straight line.

Cut the hair straight across.

11 Combine the remaining hair on the left side with some of the hair you have just cut. Holding this hair between your two fingers, and using your first cut as a guide, cut the hair in a straight line.

Combine the remaining hair on the left side with some of the cut hair.

12 To complete the straight line across the back section, combine the remaining hair on the right side with some of the cut hair. Holding this hair between your two fingers, and using the cut hair as a guide, cut the hair in a straight line.

Combine the remaining hair on the right side with some of the cut hair.

13 Check to make sure the hair length in the back section is even by pulling a little hair from each end toward the center. Do not elevate the hair. If the hair lengths do not match, trim small amounts of hair where needed to even them out, using your center cut as a guide.

Check for evenness.

14 The back section is now complete.

Completed back section.

15 Next, you will be working on the side sections. You must first layer the hair, then angle it to complete the haircut. Move to the top of the head, and separate a one-inch-wide section of hair that extends from the crown to the forehead. (Include a half inch of hair from the top of Section 3 and a half inch from Section 4.)

Separate a one-inch-wide section of hair at the top of the head.

16 Comb this section of hair between your two fingers, and include some cut hair from the back to use as your cutting guide. Hold this hair straight up.

Combine the top section of hair with some hair from the back.

17 Cut this entire piece of hair to match the guide. (The cut hair will be about three inches long. This is the shortest layer. The bottom layers will be longer.) Once you have established this center guide, you will be using it to layer the sides.

Cut the top section of hair.

18 Starting with Section 3, make a horizontal subsection about one-third of the way from the top.

Make a horizontal subsection.

19 Comb the hair straight up along with the hair you have just cut (your guide). Hold the hair between your two fingers and cut it to match the guide.

Cut the subsection to match the guide.

20 Continue to divide the hair into subsections. Comb each section up and cut the hair to match the guide. Once Section 3 is completely layered, you must angle cut the hair.

Layer the remaining subsections.

21 First, you must establish the longest side of the angle. Including some of the hair from the back as your cutting guide, comb the hair in Section 3 between your two fingers. Slide your fingers down over the ear to meet the back length.

*Combine the hair in Section 3
with some hair from the back section.*

2 Cut this hair straight across to match the hair from the back. This piece of hair that you have just cut will be referred to as your *long-side guide.*

Cut the long-side guide.

3 Next, move to the bangs at the top of this section (bangs from Section 4 can be combined here). Comb the hair between your two fingers. Holding the hair, slide your fingers down until your middle finger rests in the groove just below the eyebrows. Cut the hair at this length. This piece of hair will be referred to as your *short-side guide.*

Cut the short-side guide.

24 Now you have established your shortest length, which is at the top of this section, and your longest length, which is at the bottom. To bring these two lengths together, you are going to cut the hair between them at an angle.

The shortest and longest hair lengths.

25 Comb the hair in the front half of Section 3 forward. (Comb or clip the back section out of your way.) Including a piece of hair from the long-side guide, comb the bottom half of this section between your two fingers. Pull this hair forward and angle your fingers so they are aimed at the short-side guide. Your middle finger should be resting somewhere along the side of the nose and the center of the chin.

Angle your fingers toward the short-side guide.

26 Cut the hair between the two fingers to match the long-side guide.

Cut the hair at the bottom half of this section.

27 To finish the angle, comb the uncut hair from the top half of Section 3 between your fingers. Include a piece of hair from the short-side guide, as well as a piece of the hair you have just cut.

Comb the hair in the upper half of Section 3.

28 With your middle finger resting somewhere along the cheekbone, cut the hair to bring the two lengths together.

Cut the hair.

29 Now move to Section 4. Cut the hair in this section as you did in Section 3 (Steps 17–27). Layer the hair first, then cut your angle.

Cut the hair in Section 4.

30 Once you have cut both sides, check for evenness by combing all of the hair slightly forward. The hair should frame the face evenly. If anything looks off, correct it by going through the steps again.

The completed layered cut.

Congratulations! You have just completed the girl's layered haircut.

9. Specialty Braids, Buns, and Ponytails

The special hairstyles and styling tips presented in this chapter are specifically for girls. They are designed to make ordinary everyday hairdos look especially nice. You will find these styles particularly useful on occasions such as holidays and school picture days. (For styling tips for boys, see Dressing Up Your Son's Hair on page 89.)

I think the most important thing to remember when giving your daughter a special hairstyle, is to keep her hair as natural looking as possible. If you try to do too much, or attempt a style that is extremely different from the way she normally wears her hair, the results may not be worth the effort.

I can remember an experience I had when I was in the fourth grade. In an attempt to curl my extremely straight hair for school pictures, my mother made me wear rollers to bed the night before (something I never did). In the morning, my hair was a mess because it wouldn't hold the curl. My school picture did not reflect what I normally looked like at the time.

If your children are having pictures taken, try to make them look like themselves. For instance, if your daughter normally wears her hair up in a ponytail, make sure she wears it that way on picture day. You can always dress up the ponytail with a colorful scarf or scrungee. Better yet, for an out-of-the-ordinary ponytail variation, try an Inverted Ponytail (page 71). Simply put, give your child's everyday look a special touch. It is this image you should want the camera to capture.

Hair that is cut correctly will look good with very little effort. Most of the time, if you just wet the hair and comb it into place, you won't have to do much more. This goes for both boys and girls. In the morning, I spray my boys' hair with a little water, give them a quick combing, and send them off to school. As simple as it seems, taking these few minutes each morning to wet and comb their hair makes them look great all day.

During the winter, when the air in the house is dry, static electricity can cause hair to become flyaway. To handle this problem, first spray the hair with a little water, then use some hairspray to keep it under control. Using conditioner after washing hair is another way to combat static. Conditioner puts moisture in the hair, making the hair healthier and easier to manage.

Girls' hair can be styled and decorated in a countless number of ways. Any cut can be blown dry, giving it a new dimension (see Styling Hair With a Blow Dryer, page 70). Some styles are best worn down, while others can be worn both up and down. The one-length cut, because it has the most hair to work with, is the most versatile; it can be clipped up, pulled back, braided, or put into a ponytail.

The Pebbles Look

Named after that famous cartoon character Pebbles Flintstone, the Pebbles Look is simple to achieve and looks great. It is for one-length, angled, or layered hair.

The Pebbles Look

1 Brush the hair to make it smooth and tangle-free. Next, section the hair. Working from behind, run your thumbs from your child's ears to her crown. Brush up this section of hair.

Section off the front of the hair.

2 Tie the hair with an elastic ponytail holder to form a ponytail on top of the head.

Tie the hair into a ponytail.

3 If the child has bangs, they should be hanging down. If they have been brushed into the pony-tail, simply pull them out. Also, pull a piece of hair out of the ponytail above each ear. Let these pieces hang down.

Pull the bangs out of the ponytail, as well as a piece of hair above each ear.

4 You can leave this style as is, or choose to curl the ponytail and the hair that is hanging with a curling iron.

Curl the hair with a curling iron.

Using a Curling Iron

The curling iron is a wonderful alternative to rollers, which can take hours to work and are uncomfortable to wear. Used on dry hair, a curling iron can "spruce up" a hairstyle quickly and easily.

Although curling irons come in a variety of sizes and have different options, basically, they all work in the same way. First, the rod-shaped iron is heated up. A section of hair is then wrapped around the heated rod and held there for a few sec-onds. For soft, wavy curls with very little bend, wrap a large section of hair around the iron at one time. If tighter curls are desired, wrap smaller sections of hair around the rod. Once the hair is wrapped around the iron, hold it in place for no longer than thirty seconds. (Any longer could damage the hair.)

Also, be very careful not to let the hot iron touch the scalp or exposed skin. The extremely hot iron can easily cause a burn.

The Mini Bun

The Mini Bun is similar to the Pebbles Look (page 67) and is made almost the same way. The difference is that you will be pulling up less hair and using a barrette to secure it.

The Mini Bun

1 Brush the hair to make it smooth and tangle-free. Next, section the hair. Working from behind, run your thumbs from your child's temples to her crown. Brush up this section of hair.

Separate the front section of hair.

2 Twist this section of hair around once, then lay it down on top of the head. The twisting will cause the hair to form a little puff, which will look like a small bun on top of the head.

Lay the section on top of the head.

3 Secure the hair with a barrette, placing it flat on top of the head. The ends of the barrette should be aimed at the ears.

Secure the bun with a barrette.

Styling Hair With a Blow Dryer

*I*n order to style your daughter's hair while using a blow dryer, you will need a brush. Professionals use round brushes, which I do not recommend unless you know how to use them correctly. It is very difficult to get the hang of styling hair with a round brush without getting it caught in the hair. A flat brush, used correctly, is all you need for great results.

First, use the blow dryer to get rid of the excess wetness in the hair. When the hair is about 70 percent dry, begin styling it with the brush. Holding the brush in one hand and the blow dryer in the other, start with a section of hair in the back. Beginning at the roots, brush the hair in the desired direction. As you brush,

Brush hair in desired direction.

aim the air from the dryer on each section. The ends of the hair should go around the brush once, no more. The brush can get stuck if too much hair is rolled around it.

If your child has a one-length haircut, you might choose to brush the bottom of the hair under. If the hair is angled, you can either bend the sides under toward the face, or flip the hair back away from the face to feather it. Hair in a layered cut should be blown back away from the face on the sides and brushed under in the back. If you are working with curly hair and you want to straighten it, know that you will have to pull the hair with the brush as you blow it dry.

Once a section of hair is dry and it looks the way you want, move on to the next section. If you are drying the whole head, begin in the back and make your way to the front. If you are drying only the front, do one side and then the other. Work your way around the head until you have achieved the look you want.

When you are done drying the hair, brush through it with a stiff vent-type brush to bring it all together. If you like, keep the hair in place with a little hairspray.

The Inverted Ponytail

I believe everyone knows how to make a plain single or double ponytail. The inverted ponytail, however, is not quite as common. Easy to make, this fancy ponytail is nothing more than a simple ponytail that has been turned inside out.

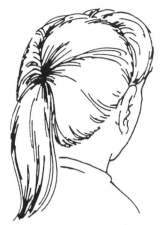

The Inverted Ponytail

1 Brush the hair smoothly into a single ponytail at the back of the head, and secure it with a ponytail holder.

Brush the hair into a single ponytail.

2 Loosen the ponytail a bit and separate the hair at the point where it goes into the holder.

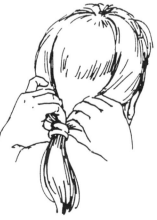

Separate the hair.

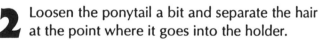

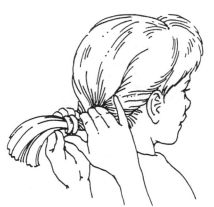

3 Using your fingers, make a hole in the hair above the ponytail holder.

Make a hole in the hair.

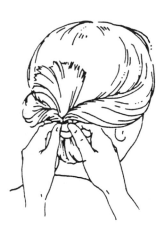

4 Put the ponytail through the hole and pull it out the bottom.

Pull the ponytail through the hole.

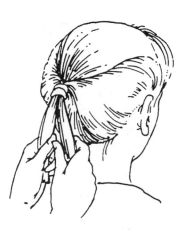

5 Tighten the ponytail by pulling it apart at the ends.

Tighten the ponytail.

The Double Braid

A simple hairstyle created by using the overbraiding technique, the Double Braid is the easiest of the braided styles presented in this chapter.

The Double Braid

1 Brush the hair to make it smooth and tangle-free. Using a comb or the end of a brush, divide the hair in half vertically down the back of the head.

Divide the hair in back.

2 You will be working with the hair on one side at a time. Divide the hair on one side into three equal-size strands.

Divide the hair into three equal strands.

3 Begin overbraiding the hair right behind the ear. Without elevating the hair, first place the right strand over the center strand (making it the new center strand).

Cross the right strand over the center strand.

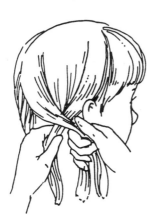

4 Next, place the left strand over the center strand.

Cross the left strand over the center strand.

5 Continue braiding the hair in this manner, alternating right and left strands into the center.

Continue braiding.

6 When you get to the end of the strands, fasten the braid with a barrette or an elastic ponytail holder.

Fasten the ends.

7 Repeat the overbraiding with the hair on the other side.

Braid the hair on the other side.

The Braided Ponytail

The Braided Ponytail is actually half French Braid (page 78) and half plain ponytail.

The Braided Ponytail

1 Brush the hair so that it is smooth and tangle-free, then brush it back away from the face. Next, separate the hair. Working from behind, run your thumbs from your child's temples to her crown. Brush this hair to smooth it, then divide this section into three equal-size strands.

Separate the front section of hair.

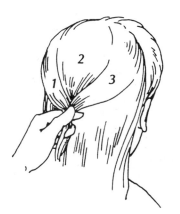

2 Begin overbraiding as you would a regular braid. First, cross the right strand into the center, then the left strand.

Begin to braid the hair at the top.

3 Before crossing the right strand over the center strand a second time, add some of the loose hair from the right side. Then cross the entire strand into the center.

Add some hair to the right strand.

4 Move to the left strand. As you did on the right side, add some hair to the strand before crossing it into the center.

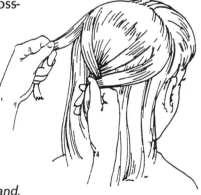

Add some hair to the left strand.

5 After you have added three strands of hair from each side, pick up the rest of the hair underneath and secure it in a ponytail.

Secure all the hair in a ponytail.

The French Braid

The French Braid begins in the same way that the Braided Ponytail (page 76) does. The only difference is that the braiding continues until there is no more hair.

The French Braid

1 Brush the hair so that it is smooth and tangle-free, then brush it back away from the face. Next, separate the hair. Working from behind, run your thumbs from your child's temples to her crown. Brush this hair to smooth it, then divide this section into three equal-size strands.

Separate the front section of hair.

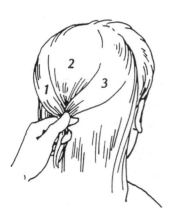

2 Begin overbraiding as you would a regular braid. First, cross the right strand into the center, then the left strand.

Begin to braid the hair at the top.

3 Before crossing the right strand over the center strand a second time, add some of the loose hair from the right side. Then cross the entire strand into the center.

Add some hair to the right strand.

4 Move to the left strand. As you did on the right side, add some hair to the strand before crossing it into the center.

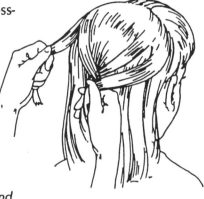

Add some hair to the left strand.

5 Continue braiding the hair in this manner, alternating right and left sides into the center. When you get to the nape of the neck, there will be no more hair to add to the strands, so just continue braiding the hair as you would a plain braid.

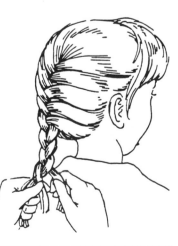

Continue braiding.

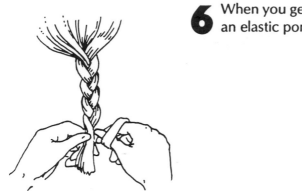

6 When you get to the end, secure the braid with an elastic ponytail holder or a barrette.

Fasten the ends.

Accessorize That Hairstyle!

Accessories play a big part in adding a special touch to a girl's hair. Headbands, clips, scarves, bows, scrungees, hair combs, and barrettes are popular items used to dress up otherwise simple hairstyles. Spruce up a plain, everyday ponytail by tying it with a scarf or bow. Use barrettes to clip hair away from your daughter's face (try twisting the hair before clipping it back). Make a colorful fashion statement by stacking two or three barrettes to hold back a section of hair. Hairdecorating possibilities are limitless. All it takes is a little imagination.

Be aware, however, that you should never use rubber bands to secure braids or ponytails; they will rip and tear the hair when you try to remove them. Instead, use material-coated elastic ponytail holders, which come in different sizes, thicknesses, and colors.

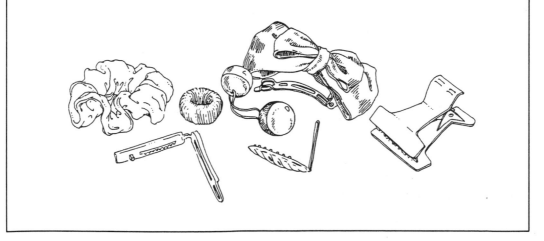

10. Boy's Wedge Haircut

The boy's wedge haircut is another name for a one-length cut. It is a very popular style because it is quick and easy to give. In addition to looking cute and neat, this cut is easy to maintain. It also makes thin hair appear thicker than it is.

This haircut looks best on a child with straight hair. Children with other hair types can also wear the wedge cut, provided the hair is not too thick. Kids with cowlicks or uncontrollable hair also look great in this style.

The hair should be clean and damp prior to cutting. If the hair is already clean, either spray it with water from your spray bottle or wet it in the tub or sink. Keep the hair damp during the haircut. If the section of hair you are working on gets dry, simply spray it with a little water.

Your work area should be in a room with a hard floor. Hair clippings are easier to sweep up than they are to vacuum. In most cases, the kitchen is the ideal spot.

INSTRUCTIONS FOR GIVING THE WEDGE HAIRCUT

Tools: Shears, • comb, • spray bottle of water (optional), • cape (optional), • hair clips (optional)

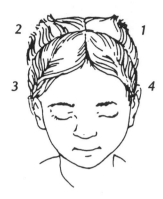

1 Divide the hair into the four basic sections, described in detail beginning on page 16. You may choose to clip up the sections or twist them away from each other.

The four basic sections.

2 Begin with the hair in Section 1. Using your comb, make a horizontal subsection about one-third of the way from the bottom of this section. (For more detailed information on subsections, refer to page 17.) Clip up (or twist) the hair on top and let the hair at the bottom hang down (you will be working on this hair first). As you have just done, make a horizontal subsection with the hair in Section 2.

Separate the back into horizontal subsections.

3 Have your child sit up straight and tilt his head forward, chin down.

Tilt the head forward.

4 Comb the hair in the center of the back section straight up, then place your middle finger horizontally on the hairline (at the nape of the neck). Let the hair hang over your middle finger, then place your forefinger on top of this hair.

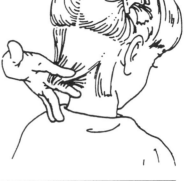

Place your middle finger at the hairline.

5 Holding both fingers against the nape of the neck, cut the hair between these fingers straight across. As you cut, hold the shears with your fingers pointing toward the ground. When you release this hair, you will see the cut line, which I will refer to as the "weight" line. This weight line will be higher than the bottom line of hair.

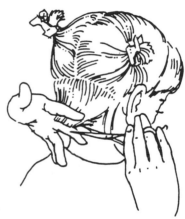

Cut the hair to form the "weight" line.

6 Using the same procedure, cut the hair to the left of the section you have just cut. Then cut the hair to the right. Comb the hair straight down. You will see two distinct lines—the weight line and the line across the bottom length of hair, which will be long and shaggy.

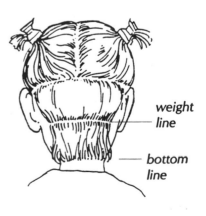

weight line

bottom line

Two hair lines—the weight line and the bottom line.

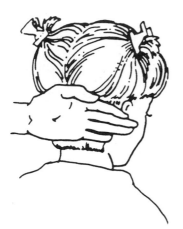

7 To straighten the bottom line, place the back of your hand against the child's head, and hold your pinkie finger horizontally at the desired length. *Remember. The bottom line you are about to cut is not supposed to match the weight line. The idea of this haircut is to have two separate lengths.*

*Hold your pinkie finger horizontally
at the desired length of the bottom line.*

8 Holding the shears horizontally with your fingertips pointing toward the ground, follow your pinkie and cut a straight line across the center of this section.

Cut the hair across the center of the back section.

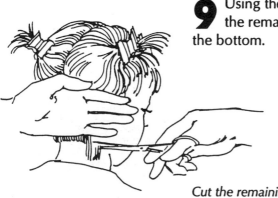

9 Using the hair you have just cut as a guide, cut the remaining hair to form a straight line across the bottom.

*Cut the remaining hair
to form a straight bottom line.*

10 You have cut a straight line across the bottom of the hair, as well as a weight line into the back of the hair. You should be able to tell which line is which. You will be using the weight line as a guide to cut the rest of the hair in the back section.

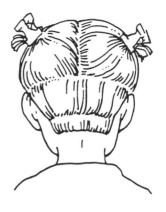

The weight line and the completed bottom line.

11 Take the hair that is clipped up in Section 1 and divide it in half horizontally. Let the hair at the bottom hang down, and reclip the hair at the top. Do the same thing with the hair in Section 2. The hair that is hanging will be longer than the hair at the weight line.

Further divide the back into subsections.

12 Comb the center section of hair between your forefinger and middle finger. *Do not include hair below the weight line.* Holding the shears with your fingers pointing toward the ground, cut this hair to match the length of the weight line (your cutting guide). Do not elevate the hair as you cut.

Cut the center section of hair to match the weight line.

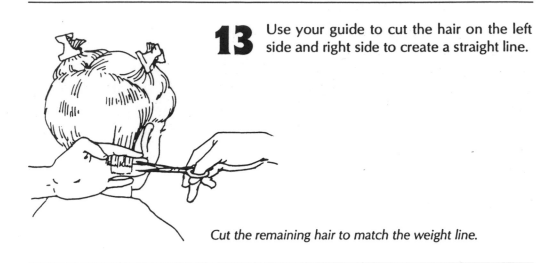

13 Use your guide to cut the hair on the left side and right side to create a straight line.

Cut the remaining hair to match the weight line.

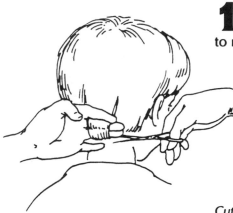

14 Let down the rest of the hair in the back sections. As you have just done, cut this hair to match the length of the weight line.

Cut the hair in the last subsection.

15 The back section is now complete.

The completed back section.

16 Move to the hair in Section 3. (Unless your child's hair is very thick, he will not need subsections.) Comb the hair that is above the ear between your forefinger and middle finger. Hold these fingers at the hairline above the ear. Do not include any hair from the back section. Cut a straight line across to establish a length on the side. After you have made the cut, comb the hair down (without holding it in your fingers) and trim any hair that is not in line.

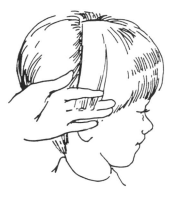

Cut a straight line at the hairline above the ear.

17 To cut bangs, move to the front of the head. Hair from Section 4 can be included here. Comb the center of the bangs between your forefinger and middle finger (include hair that extends from the center of the forehead to the outside of the eyebrow). Bring your fingers down to the desired bang length. Holding the shears horizontally with your fingertips pointing toward the ground, cut the hair straight across.

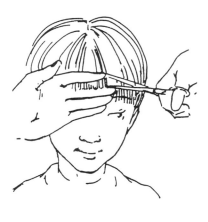

Cut the bangs.

18 Now you are going to connect the hair that is between the bangs and the ear by cutting it at an angle. First comb the hair forward. Place your two fingers around this hair. Include some of the hair from the bangs as well as some of the hair from the line over the ear to use as cutting guides. Cut the hair to form the front angle.

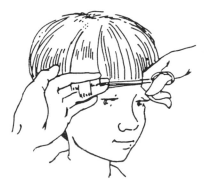

Cut the hair to form the front angle.

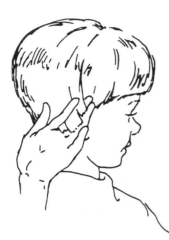

19 Now blend the side and back lengths together. Do this in much the same way that you blended the side and front lengths in Step 18. Comb the hair from behind the ear forward. Slip your two fingers around this hair. Include some hair from above the ear as well as some from the weight line. Cut the hair to connect the lengths. Do not shorten the weight line, simply cut off a bit of the corner to blend.

Connect the side and back lengths.

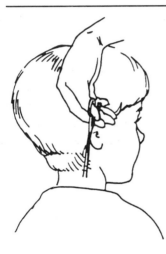

20 Comb the hair straight down. Blend the weight line with the bottom line.

Blend the weight line with the bottom line.

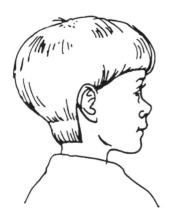

21 Now move to Section 4. Cut the hair in this section as you did in Section 3 (Steps 16–20). When you have cut both sides, look at your child straight on to make sure the sides are even. Use his ears to judge.

The completed wedge cut.

Congratulations! You have just completed the boy's wedge cut.

Dressing Up Your Son's Hair

There will always be those special occasions—holidays, parties, weddings, school picture days, etc.—when you will want your son's hair to look especially nice. Unfortunately, boys usually don't have a lot of hair to work with, and there is only so much you can do to dress it up. One of the things I do, especially on occasions when pictures are going to be taken, is add some styling gel to just-washed hair.

A versatile hair-care product, gel mainly helps keep hair in place. Applied to damp hair, gel gives hair a "wet look." If you desire the hold, but not the "wet look," simply brush out the hair once the gel has dried.

When using gel, dab a very small amount—no bigger than the size of a dime—in the palm of your hand. Rub your hands together, then run them through the damp hair to distribute the gel evenly. If necessary, apply extra gel on cowlicks or other areas that may require more hold. If you have applied the gel but feel you still need more, wet your hands with a little water from a spray bottle and use the gel that remains on your hands before taking more from the tube.

Another way you can give your son's hair a special look is by blowing it dry. Start with clean damp hair and blow it back away from the face. Using a flat brush (a vented air brush works best) brush the hair in the desired direction while following it with the air from a blow dryer. Once the hair is dry, rub a dab of styling gel between your hands and run it through the hair. Using gel on dry hair results in a different, more sophisticated look than it does on wet hair.

*Brush the hair straight back
while blowing it dry.*

11. Boy's Layered Haircut

For centuries, boys have worn the layered cut in one variation or another. This most popular hairstyle is not the easiest one to give, but once you have tried it a few times, it will become easier.

I have given instructions for a basic layered cut. The hair length is off-the-collar in the back and above the ears on the sides. The hair on the sides can either be combed back or down. The hair on top can be brushed off the forehead or left as bangs. It is truly a classic haircut that never goes out of style.

One of the beauties of this cut is that it looks good on anyone, no matter what the hair type. Once hair is layered, even the wildest tresses seem to fall into place. The one thing you should keep in mind, however, is that some boys have a growth pattern at the crown of their head that causes the hair to stick up when it is cut too short. If your child's hair is like this, simply leave the crown area slightly longer than suggested in the instructions.

The hair should be clean and damp prior to cutting. If the hair is already clean, either spray it with water from your spray bottle or wet it in the tub or sink. Keep the hair damp during the haircut. If the section of hair you are working on gets dry, simply spray it with a little water.

Your work area should be in a room with a hard floor. Hair clippings are easier to sweep up than they are to vacuum. In most cases, the kitchen is the ideal spot.

INSTRUCTIONS FOR GIVING THE BOY'S LAYERED HAIRCUT

Tools: Shears, • comb, • spray bottle of water (optional), • cape (optional)

1 Divide the hair into the four basic sections, described in detail beginning on page 16. You can simply comb and separate the sections; hair clips are not necessary.

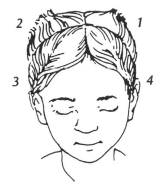

The four basic sections.

2 Starting with the hair in Section 1, make a vertical subsection near the center of the back of the head. (For more detailed information on subsections, refer to page17.) Comb the hair straight out from the head at a 90° angle.

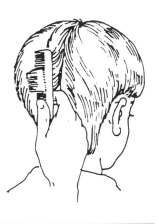

Comb the subsection straight out.

3 With the palm of your hand facing you, place your forefinger and middle finger around the hair at the bottom of this subsection. Pull the hair toward you, until the back of your fingers is about an inch from the child's head. (If any hair from the top of this subsection gets in your way, push it up and onto the crown of the head.)

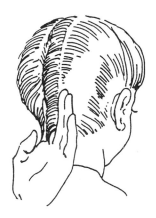

Place your forefinger and middle finger around the hair.

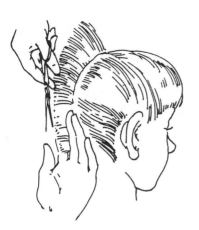

4 Using your middle finger as a guide, cut this section of hair. As you cut, rest the bottom of the shears on your middle finger.

Cut the hair at the bottom of the section.

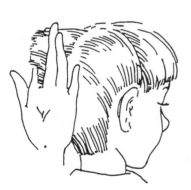

5 Next, move your two fingers up and place them around the remaining hair at the top of this subsection. Include a little of the hair you have just cut. As you did before, pull your two fingers away from the crown of the head, gradually making the hair near the crown longer. Once again, using your middle finger as a guide, cut this hair. This center subsection will be your cutting guide for the back layers.

Cut the hair at the top of the section.

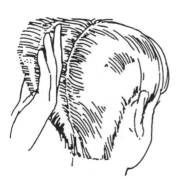

6 Make another vertical subsection next to the one you have just cut. Starting at the bottom of this section, comb the hair between your two fingers and include the hair you have just cut as a guide. Slide your fingers away from the head and cut the hair to match the guide. Cut the top half of this subsection in the same way.

Cut the next section,
using your first cut as a guide.

7 Following the same simple procedure, cut the remaining hair in Section 1.

A *word of caution*—be sure you can see your guide before cutting any hair. Don't try to guess where the guide is. If you have difficulty seeing your guide, make smaller subsections. Also, remember to hold the hair in each subsection straight out before cutting—don't drag the hair to one side or the other.

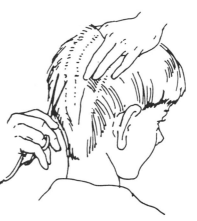

Cut the remaining subsections.

8 Move to Section 2. Use the same procedure to layer the hair in this section (Steps 2–7).

Layer the hair in Section 2.

9 Once you have layered the back sections, you will be cutting a straight line across the bottom. Have your child sit up straight and tilt his head forward with his chin down. He will have to maintain this position for you to cut the back correctly.

Tilt head forward.

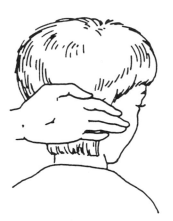

10 To cut the bottom line, place the back of your hand against the child's head and hold your pinkie finger horizontally at the desired length.

*Hold your pinkie finger horizontally
at the desired length of the bottom line.*

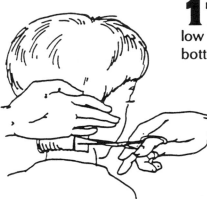

11 Holding the shears horizontally with your fingertips pointing toward the ground, follow your pinkie and cut a straight line across the bottom of this center section.

Cut the hair across the center of the back section.

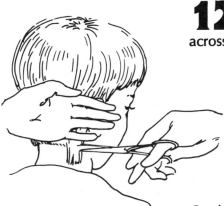

12 Using the hair you have just cut as a guide, cut the remaining hair to form a straight line across the bottom.

Cut the remaining hair across the bottom.

13 Next you will be layering the side sections. Move to the top of the head and separate a one-inch-wide section of hair that extends from the crown to the forehead. (Include a half inch of hair from the top of Section 3 and a half inch from Section 4.) Once this section of hair is cut, you will be using it as a guide to layer the hair on both sides.

Separate a one-inch-wide section of hair at the top of the head.

14 Comb this section of hair between your two fingers, and include some hair from the back to use as your cutting guide. Hold this hair straight up.

Combine the top section of hair with some hair from the back.

15 Cut this entire section of hair to match the piece of hair from the back. (It will be easier to make a straight line if you stand at your child's side as you cut.) You will be using this center section as a cutting guide to layer the sides.

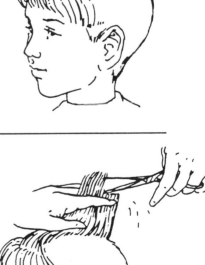

Cut the top section of hair.

16 To layer the rest of Section 3, you will be working with vertical subsections. (For more information on subsections, refer to page 17.) Start with the hair above the ear. Comb this section of hair away from the child's head and slip your two fingers around it. Include a little hair from the back section, as well as some hair from the top section that you have just cut, to use as guides.

Separate the hair into the first vertical subsection.

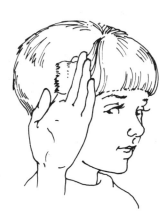

17 Cut the hair to match the guides.

Cut the hair to match the guides.

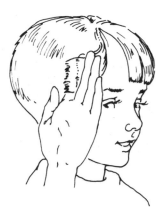

18 Continue layering the rest of Section 3 in this manner, moving forward with each subsection. If the front of the hair is mostly bangs, when you get to the front (the last subsection), pull the hair back slightly before cutting it. This will keep the bangs long enough.

Cut the remaining hair in Section 3.

19 Once you have layered the side, you must cut the hair around the ears. Comb down the hair that is above the ears and hold it between your two fingers. Hold this hair as close to the head as you can in order achieve a nice short length. Cut the hair under your index finger straight across. As you cut, the shears should be resting on your middle finger. Let go of the hair and comb it again. Trim any hair that is not up to the line above the ear.

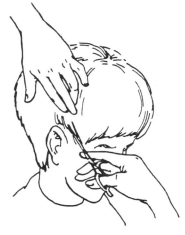

Trim the hair around the ears.

20 To blend the side length with the back, comb the hair from behind the ear forward. Slip your two fingers around this hair. Include some hair from the back, as well as some hair from above the ear. Angle your fingers and cut the hair to blend the two lengths.

Blend the back and side lengths.

21 To cut the bangs, comb the hair in the center of the forehead between your two fingers. Slide your fingers down to the desired bang length, and cut the hair straight across.

Cut the bangs.

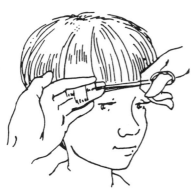

22 To blend the bang length with the side length, comb the hair that is in front of the ear forward and hold it between your two fingers. Include a piece of hair from the bangs and a piece from the side. Angle your fingers and cut the hair to blend the two lengths.

Blend the bangs and side length.

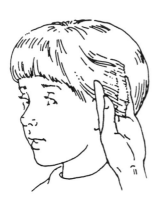

23 Move to Section 4. Use the same procedure to layer and finish the hair in this section (Steps 16–22).

Layer the hair in Section 4.

24 When you have finished cutting the hair on both sides, look at your child straight on to check for evenness. Trim bits of hair where necessary.

The completed haircut.

Congratulations! You have just completed the boy's layered haircut.

12. Boy's Buzz Cut

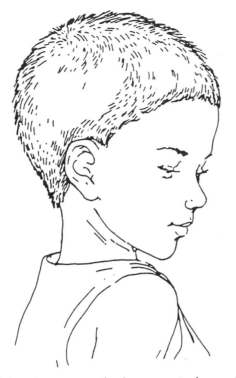

Also called the clipper cut, the buzz cut is the easiest of the boy's haircuts to give. It doesn't take a lot of time or talent to get a nice-looking style. Hair clippers rather than shears are used to cut the hair, resulting in a style that is much shorter than others. It is perfect for boys who are active in sports. Although there are many hairstyles that can be done using hair clippers, the one I have presented is for the basic buzz cut.

You can give a buzz cut to children with any hair type. The style is short and easy to care for. You may not even have to comb the hair in the morning for it look good! Another advantage of this haircut is that you probably won't need to cut the hair again for a couple of months.

As mentioned in Chapter 1, basic hair clippers come with four attachments. We will be using attachment number 2, which cuts hair to a 1/2-inch length, and attachment number 3, for cutting hair to a 3/4-inch length. For more detailed information on hair clippers, see pages 7 and 8.

The hair should be clean and damp prior to cutting. If the hair is already clean, either spray it with water from your spray bottle or wet it in the tub or sink. Keep the hair damp during the haircut. If the section of hair you are working on gets dry, simply spray it with a little water.

Your work area should be in a room with a hard floor. Hair clippings are easier to sweep up than they are to vacuum. In most cases, the kitchen is the ideal spot.

INSTRUCTIONS FOR GIVING THE BUZZ CUT

Tools: Hair clippers and attachment numbers 2 and 3, • shears, • comb, • spray bottle of water (optional), • cape (optional)

1 Divide the hair into the four basic sections, described in detail beginning on page 16. Simply comb and separate the sections; hair clips are not necessary.

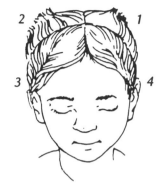

The four basic sections.

2 Comb the hair in Sections 3 and 4 forward and out of your way. (If the hair is already short, it may not separate into sections. If this is the case, just be aware of where the sections are.)

Comb the side sections forward.

3 Snap attachment number 2 onto the clippers.

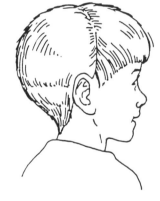

Snap on the attachment.

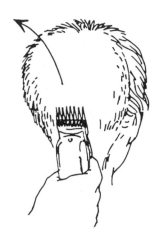

4 Begin with the hair in the center of the back section. Whisk the clippers up from the nape of the neck to the crown. As you move the clippers up, the attachment should be resting on the head. Be sure to lift the clippers off the head as it comes over the curve of the occipital bone. Leave the hair on top uncut.

*Whisk the clippers up
from the nape of the neck to the crown.*

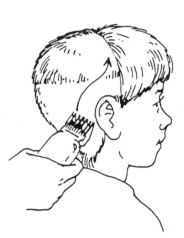

5 Moving to the left, continue to cut the remaining hair in Section 1.

Cut the remaining hair in Section 1.

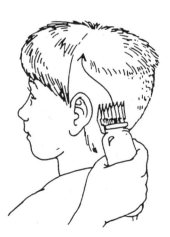

6 Using the same procedure, cut the hair in Section 2.

Cut the hair in Section 2.

7 Next, move to Section 3 (right side). Using the same motion as you did in the back, start with the hair above the ear. Whisk the clippers up, lifting it off at the curve. Leave the top uncut. Cut around the ear as evenly as you can. You will be trimming the "fringe" around the ear later.

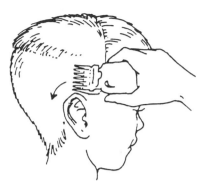

Trim around the ear.

8 Move to Section 4 (left side). Use the same procedure that was used in Step 7 to cut the hair in this section.

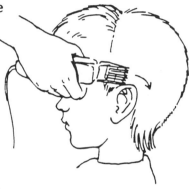

Cut the hair in Section 4.

9 Now go back and run the clippers over any area in which the hair is longer than the rest. You can run the clippers back to front, front to back, side to side, or whatever direction is necessary to cut the hair to an even length. (You will probably need to do this to the hair around the ears.)

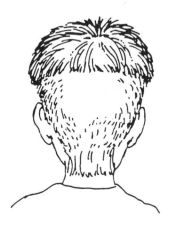

Make sure back and sides are evenly clipped.

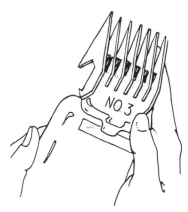

10 Turn off the clippers, remove the attachment, and snap on attachment number 3. You will be using this to cut the top section of hair.

Snap on attachment number 3.

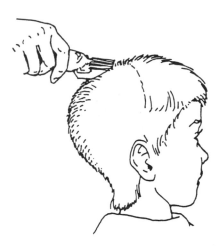

11 Starting in the back, cut the crown area completely. Keep the attachment against the head as you clip.

Cut the hair in the crown area.

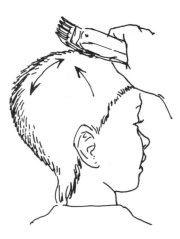

12 Next, cut the hair on top of the head. Starting at the forehead, run the clippers from the front of the head to the back. Be sure to hold the attachment against the head as you move it around the curves. (You can move the clippers from back to front, front to back, or side to side; it doesn't matter. However, clippers cut best when they move against the natural growth pattern of the hair.)

Cut the hair on top.

13 As you did with the bottom and side sections, check the top area for any pieces of hair you might have missed. Use the clippers to even out the hair.

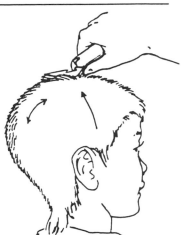

Even out the hair on top.

14 Now you will be using your shears to trim the fringe around the ears and to straighten the bottom line in the back. To make a straight bottom line, have your child put his head forward, chin down.

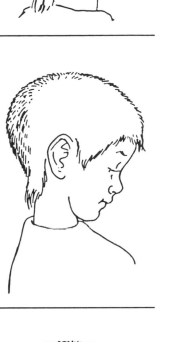

Tilt the head forward.

15 Comb the hair down. Place the back of your hand against the child's head, and hold your pinkie finger horizontally at the desired length.

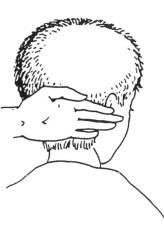

Hold your pinkie finger horizontally at the desired length of the bottom line.

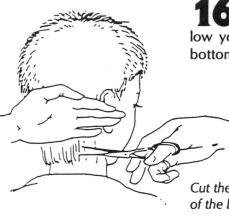

16 Holding the shears horizontally with your fingertips pointing toward the ground, follow your pinkie and cut a straight line across the bottom of this center section.

Cut the hair across the center of the back section.

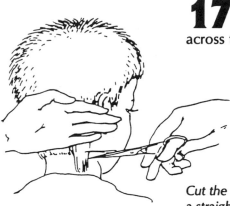

17 Using the hair you have just cut as a guide, cut the remaining hair to form a straight line across the bottom.

Cut the remaining hair to form a straight bottom line.

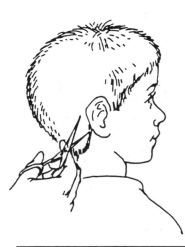

18 Trim the hair around the ears, if there is any. Cut the hair from behind the ears down to the length of hair in back.

Trim the hair behind the ear.

19 Comb the hair in the bang area between your forefinger and middle finger. Trim this hair a little.

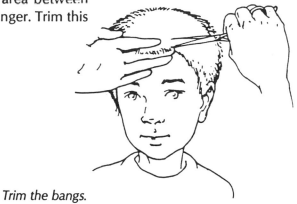

Trim the bangs.

20 Comb the hair on the sides forward. Trim this hair at an angle that extends from the front of the ears to the bangs.

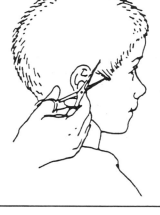

Angle the sides.

21 Check the hair that frames the face. Trim any uneven hairs.

Check for evenness.

Congratulations! You have just completed the boy's buzz cut.

13. Remedies for Children's Experimentation

C hildren's experimentation" is a term I use to describe those little haircuts that kids give themselves or their siblings. I have seen these often-disastrous cuts time and again throughout my years as a hairstylist. I have also discovered a few preventive measures for experimentation, as well as a few ways to fix (even if minimally) an already-damaged hairstyle.

I have found that children who are most apt to cut hair (either their own or someone else's) are usually around four years old. Preschool-age children are at a point in their lives where they are developing many different skills. Psychologically, they are learning to be independent and initiate activities on their own. Physically, their small-motor skills are improving. These skills include the use of scissors, which is great fun for many four-year-olds. Unfortunately, a young child's judgement is not always very good, so you can expect small disasters when your child decides to get creative with a pair of scissors.

There are some measures you can take to prevent your child from giving himself, a sibling, or even the dog a haircut. The best thing is probably the most obvious—keep all scissors out of your child's reach. Allow the use of scissors only when you can sit down and work with your child. Get him or her a pair of safety scissors, and don't forget to say that the scissors are for cutting paper only. Sit with your child and show him or her the proper way to hold scissors. Give the child things to cut (old magazines are good). Never let your child use haircutting shears. Aside from the obvious physical danger, using haircutting shears to cut paper even once can dull the blades.

If your child expresses a desire to cut hair, you might lessen the temptation by giving him or her an old doll you might have lying around. Allowing your child to cut a doll's hair may be all it takes to help curb the desire. I'm not telling you to suggest this idea, but if your child wants to give a haircut, letting him or her experiment on a doll might be a good idea. Of course, you should assist the child as he or she cuts away. I have a friend who remembers cutting her doll's hair when she was a very young girl. After the haircut, she decided she didn't like her doll anymore because it looked "ruined." This experience satisfied her desire to cut the hair on any of her other dolls. It also prevented her from experimenting with her own hair.

My own children have a collection of "trolls," which are little dolls with funny faces and lots of long wispy hair. One night, the babysitter allowed the children to give haircuts to all nine of their trolls. I must admit, I was surprised when I came home and saw their troll collection lined up on the shelf, each doll with a Mohawk haircut. My kids were proud and pleased with their work. The experience didn't hurt anyone and it helped them get the urge to cut hair out of their system. Since that night, my children have had no desire to give another doll a haircut.

Of course, allowing children to give dolls haircuts will not necessarily stop them from wanting to cut more. It does, however, satisfy the curiosity of many children, so it may be worth it to give this idea a try.

Children want to be able to do everything. Cutting hair, like driving a car, takes knowledge and instruction. Whenever my children express the desire to cut hair (on real people, not dolls), I tell them that they will be able to do so when they are old enough to do it correctly. "Someday" or "When you are older" is a positive response to a child. It helps them understand that although they cannot give haircuts now, they will be able to sometime in the future.

It is best to discuss the topic of haircutting with your child when you are actually giving him or her a haircut. Talk about such things as the sharpness of the shears, explaining how dangerous they can be when not held or used properly. Explain to your child that people must learn the correct way to cut hair before they do any actual cutting.

Having discussions with your child, as well as taking precautionary measures such as allowing him or her to cut a doll's hair, can be helpful in discouraging him or her from giving haircuts. Sometimes, however, no matter how many precautions you take to avoid this undesirable behavior, a child might somehow get a hold of a pair of scissors and give himself or a sibling a haircut. If this happens, all you can do is try to make the hair look as decent as possible until the "mistake" grows in. Following are the most common haircutting experimentation areas and possible remedies.

THE BANGS

The bang area, because it is the easiest to reach, is the spot most often cut by children. If your child has cut his or her bangs, there are steps you can take to possibly make this bad situation a little better.

First, section off a pie-shaped bang section (page 25, Step 1). Following the remaining directions, trim the bangs a little shorter than you normally like them. Try to get the short pieces that your child has cut even with the new length. If there are extremely short pieces, however, leave them alone. Don't cut any of the remaining bangs to match the very short pieces. Instead, cut whatever long bang hair is left just above the eyebrows and leave it at that length. You will have to wait until the shorter bangs grow to match the rest.

Layering the bang section is another alternative for blending the shorter pieces with the rest of the bangs. Directions for layering bangs are found on page 27.

One last option for remedying "butchered" bangs is to chip

Chip out the bangs.

the bangs out in an attempt to give them a wispy look. First comb the bangs between your forefinger and middle finger. Slide your fingers to the longest possible length. Using the tips of your shears, chip away tiny pieces of hair (see illustration). Chip the hair that is found in the thickest area to best even out the bangs.

THE TOP SECTION

Sometimes a child will simply hold up some hair on the top of his or her head and cut it off. If your child has a one-length hairstyle, and he or she has cut only a small piece, you can probably leave the hair alone until the cut piece grows back.

If a substantial amount of hair has been cut from the top, it is best to layer the hair to blend the "mistake" with the rest of the hair. For girls, follow the instructions for the layered haircut found in Chapter 8; for boys, refer to Chapter 11. Keep in mind that the top layer can be only as short as two inches or so. Hair that is shorter will stick up everywhere. If there are pieces of hair that have been cut this short, just leave them alone. Eventually, the short pieces will grow in to blend with the rest. If the hair has been cut to an extremely short length on a boy, you could try giving him the buzz cut found in Chapter 12.

THE SIDES

If your child has cut some hair from the side of his head, you must try to even out this section.

The first thing you must do is separate the hair into the four basic sections described beginning on page 16. Comb the two back sections out of your way for now. You can clip them back if you prefer. Comb the hair on the "cut side" down over the ear. Slip this hair between your forefinger and middle finger. Slide these fingers down to a length that will blend with some of the cut hair. Cut the hair that you are holding to make a straight line, angling it up to the bangs. If your child does not have bangs, you may want to cut some, depending on how short the side is. If your child has bangs, blend them with the side length by cutting the hair between these two lengths at an angle (see illustration).

Now move to the other side and comb the hair down between your two fingers. Slide your fingers down to the same

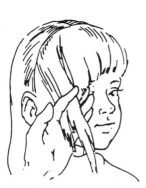

Cut the hair at an angle to blend the side length with the bangs.

length as the hair on the other side and cut the hair. Now comb the hair on this side forward and slip it between your two fingers. As you did on the other side, cut the hair at an angle to blend the side length with the bangs. Try to cut the hair on both sides so they match.

THE BACK LENGTH

If your child has cut some hair from the back length, you have two options, depending on how much hair has been cut— either make the entire back length shorter, or round off the back section to make the length appear more even.

If you choose to make the entire back length shorter, follow the instructions for the haircut that your child has. For instance, if your son has a layered cut, turn to Chapter 11, and follow the steps that describe how to cut the back section of this hairstyle.

If you choose to round the bottom of the back section (the popular choice for girls with long hair), begin by separating the hair into the four basic sections described on page 16. These sections will give you points by which to judge. Beginning at the center of the back section, cut the hair to the right and left, angling it slightly shorter as you cut toward each end. Check for evenness by pulling the end pieces of hair from each side together in the back (see illustration). If necessary, the side sections should be cut so they are even with the back.

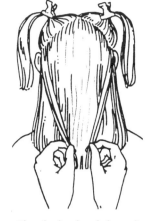

Check the back length for evenness.

ALL AROUND

If your child has cut his or her hair in different areas, I suggest you read this entire chapter, then give your child a complete haircut. Turn to the chapter that offers directions for the haircut your child normally has. Of course, you will have to alter the steps slightly, depending on the location of the cut areas.

Use the suggestions from this chapter to deal with crucial areas, like the bangs. In general, try to cut the hair to a length that looks good; don't cut it all off! Some of the cut pieces will probably be too short to blend with the rest of the hair. In this case, cut the hair that is long enough and don't worry about the hair that is too short. The illustration shows a piece of hair that is too short to cut. It also shows where to cut the surrounding hair in order to bring the lengths a little closer together.

Where to cut hair that surrounds a very short piece.

WHEN THERE IS NO HOPE

I'll never forget the worst case of "child experimentation" I have ever seen. A little boy had gotten hold of his father's beard trimmer and shaved the entire top and part of one side of his sister's head. The only way I could have made her hair even would have been to shave her entire head, which was out of the question. I was able to save some hair by layering what she had left. When the shaved area grew, the new growth blended with the layers. By no means did that little girl look good when she left the salon, but after a short length of time, the shaved part of her head began to grow and blend with the rest of her hair.

Making "mistake-cut" hair look good immediately is impossible most of the time. Creating a shape for the hair to grow into is often the most you can do. Keep in mind that hair grows an average of a half inch a month. So be patient and know that it may take a little time, but eventually the hair will grow back.

Conclusion

Well, there you have it—all the information necessary to give your child a great-looking haircut at home. You now know the proper tools to use, the best style for your child's particular hair type, and tips and guidelines to make the experience a pleasurable one for both you and your child. The illustrated step-by-step instructions will help guide you through each haircut with ease and confidence.

Pat yourself on the back and remember to maintain a positive attitude with each haircutting attempt. Your efficiency and confidence will increase with each cut you give. Good luck!

Index

Other Interesting Books Available From Avery Publishing Group

All of these exciting parenting books are available at your local bookseller. For a free copy of our complete catalog of books, write us at 120 Old Broadway, Garden City Park, New York 11040, or call us at 1-800-548-5757.

SMART MEDICINE FOR A HEALTHIER CHILD
A Practical A-to-Z Reference to Natural and Conventional Treatments for Infants and Children
Janet Zand, Rachel Walton, and Robert Rountree

Written by a medical doctor, a naturopath, and a nurse, *Smart Medicine for a Healthier Child* is the definitive up-to-date A-to-Z guide to the most common childhood illnesses, disorders, and injuries and their treatments using both alternative and conventional medicine. This easy-to-use book is divided into 3 parts. In addition to conventional treatments, Part 1 discusses herbal and homeopathic remedies, acupressure, diet, and nutritional supplements as they apply to healing. Part 2 is an alphabetical listing of the various health problems affecting children. Part 3 provides a detailed look at the therapies suggested in Part 2.

Trade Paperback, $17.95

HOW TO TEACH YOUR BABY TO READ
Glenn Doman

Glenn Doman has demonstrated, time and time again, that very young children are far more capable of learning than we ever imagined. He has taken his remarkable work—work that explores why children from birth to age six learn better and faster than older children do—and given it practical application. As the founder of The Institutes for the Achievement of Human Potential, he has created several in-home programs that any parent can follow. *How to Teach Your Baby to Read* is the classic book that for almost thirty years has brought parents and their babies closer together.

How to Teach Your Baby to Read explains how to begin and expand a reading program, how to make and organize your materials, and how to more fully develop your child's potential.

Trade Paperback, $9.95

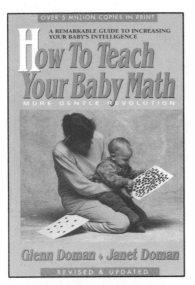

HOW TO TEACH YOUR BABY MATH
Glenn Doman

Written for parents, *How to Teach Your Baby Math* presents a revolutionary idea: that children are far more capable of learning than we had ever dreamed, that we have been wasting our children's most important years by refusing to allow them to learn when it is easiest for them to do so. *How to Teach Your Baby Math* instructs you in successfully developing your child's ability to think and reason. It explains how to begin and expand a math program, how to make and organize your materials, and how to more fully develop your child's potential.

Trade Paperback, $9.95

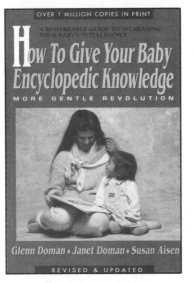

HOW TO GIVE YOUR BABY ENCYCLOPEDIC KNOWLEDGE
Glenn Doman

How to Give Your Baby Encyclopedic Knowledge provides a program of visually stimulating information designed to expand your child's potential as well as enrich his or her life. It shows just how easy and pleasurable it is to teach a young child about the arts, science, nature, and more. It explains how to begin and expand your program, how to make and organize your materials, and how to more fully develop your child's mind.

Trade Paperback, $9.95

HOW TO MULTIPLY YOUR BABY'S INTELLIGENCE
Glenn Doman and Janet Doman

Learning begins at birth, or maybe earlier, say the authors—and not when formal education begins at age six. *How to Multiply Your Baby's Intelligence* draws upon more than a half-century of work to show clearly that tiny children can learn virtually anything that we teach them in an honest, factual, and joyful way. Glenn Doman and his daughter, Janet, detail the programs developed at The Institutes for the Achievement of Human Potential—programs designed to expand your child's overall intellectual development. Learning to read, mastering mathematics, or gaining knowledge of any subject need not be chores for either the parent or the child. Instead, they can be a source of fun, enjoyment, and pride.

Trade Paperback, $12.95